ANCIENT RUINS
OF THE SOUTHWEST

ANCIENT RUINS
OF THE SOUTHWEST

An Archaeological Guide
by David Grant Noble

Northland Press · Flagstaff, Arizona

The photographs, unless otherwise noted, are by the author.

All maps are current in 1981.

Permission rights have been granted for the use of material from the following sources:

Adolph Bandelier's Final Report of Investigations Among the Indians of the Southwestern United States, Carried on Mainly in the Years 1880 – 1885, Part II. Papers of the Archaeological Institute Of America, American Series IV.

Kino's Historical Memoir of Pimeria Alta, by Herbert Eugene Bolton. The Arthur H. Clark Company, 1919.

The Professor's House, by Willa Cather. Alfred A. Knopf, Inc., New York, 1925.

The Dominguez-Escalante Journal, translated by Fray Angelico Chavez. Brigham Young University Press, 1976.

Aztec Ruins National Monument – New Mexico, by John M. Corbett. National Park Service Historical Handbook, Series No. 36, Washington, D.C., 1962.

Cycles of Conquest: The Impact of Spain, Mexico, and the United States on Indians of the Southwest, 1533 – 1960, by Edward H. Spicer. University of Arizona Press, 1962.

The Southwestern Journals of Adolph F. Bandelier, 1880 – 1882. University of New Mexico Press, 1966.

The Missions of New Mexico, 1776, A Description by Fray Francisco Atanasio Dominguez, translated by Eleanor B. Adams and Fray Angelico Chavez. University of New Mexico Press, 1966.

Land of Poco Tiempo, Charles F. Lummis. University of New Mexico Press, 1966 edition.

Gran Quivira: Excavations in a 17th-Century Jumano Pueblo, by Gordon Vivian. Archaeological Research Series Number Eight, National Park Service, U.S. Department of the Interior, 1964.

A Colony on the Move: Gaspar Castano de Sosa's Journal, 1590 – 1591, by Albert H. Schroeder and Dan Matson. School of American Research, 1965.

Frontispiece: Gila Cliff Dwellings
Front Cover: Montezuma Castle

To my parents, who introduced me to
the fascination of ancient ruins

Contents

PREFACE   ix

THE MOGOLLON: Roots of Southwestern Culture   5

Gila Cliff Dwellings National Monument   7
Three Rivers Petroglyph Site   10
Casas Grandes   12

THE HOHOKAM: Desert Farmers and Craftsmen   15

Casa Grande Ruins National Monument   18
The Hardy Site   21
Pueblo Grande Ruins   22

THE ANASAZI: From Prehistory to the Present   25

Mesa Verde National Park   31
Ute Mountain Ute Tribal Park   35
Hovenweep National Monument   37
Lowry Pueblo Ruins   39
Escalante and Dominguez Ruins   41
Three Kiva Pueblo   43
Newspaper Rock   45
Canyonlands National Park   47
Edge of the Cedars State Historical Monument   50
Westwater Ruin   51
Mule Canyon Indian Ruins   53
Natural Bridges National Monument   53
Anasazi Indian Village State Historical Monument   55
Navajo National Monument   57
Sand Island Petroglyph Site   61
Grand Canyon National Park   62
Grand Gulch   67
Canyon de Chelly National Monument   69
Kin-Li-Chee Tribal Park   73
Kinishba Ruins   74
Petrified Forest National Park   75
Chaco Culture National Historical Park   76
Aztec Ruins National Monument   83
Salmon Ruins   86

Casamero Ruins   89
Village of the Great Kivas   90
Hawikuh   92
El Morro National Monument   95

THE SINAGUA: Anasazi Frontiers   99

Wupatki National Monument   101
Walnut Canyon National Monument   104
Tuzigoot National Monument   105
Montezuma Castle National Monument   107
Montezuma Well   111

THE SALADO   113

Tonto National Monument   113
Besh Ba Gowah Ruins   116

PUEBLOS AND MISSIONS OF THE RIO GRANDE   117

Bandelier National Monument   122
Puyé Cliff Dwellings   128
Indian Petroglyphs State Park   131
Coronado State Monument   133
Pecos National Monument   135
Jemez State Monument   140
Salinas National Monument   142
    Abo   142
    Quarai   144
    Gran Quivira   146
The Cerrito Site   149
Sandia Cave   150

THE FUTURE OF ANTIQUITY IN THE SOUTHWEST   153

ARCHAEOLOGICAL RESOURCES PROTECTION ACT OF 1979   155

MAPS

Ancient Ruins of the Southwest   2, 3
Four Corners Area   24
Mesa Verde National Park   34
Hovenweep National Monument   38
Chaco Culture National Historical Park   77
Sinagua and Salado Areas   97
Wupatki National Monument   98
Rio Grande Area   119
Bandelier National Monument   123

Preface

No region of this continent and few areas of the world can boast a collection of archaeological ruins equal to that of the American Southwest. Due to unique geologic features and an arid climate, this vast expanse of mountains, deserts, and canyon-cut plateaus often has provided ideal environments for preserving even the most fragile artifacts.

It is to our considerable fortune that over the past hundred years, a few far-sighted and influential individuals recognized the extraordinary cultural heritage of the Southwest and successfully campaigned to have certain archaeological treasures set aside as public monuments. These preserves comprise a far-flung and sometimes spectacular outdoor museum. They also represent but the gleaming tip of an iceberg under whose waterline lie archaeological sites numbering in the scores of thousands. Blessed with such resources, it is possible for us today to see and understand the Southwest through its prehistory.

The area we know today as New Mexico, Arizona, southern Utah, and southern Colorado has sheltered and nurtured human beings for at least twelve thousand years, possibly much longer. Since the 1880s, archaeologists have displayed a consuming interest in trying to unravel the long complex history of these early people. The Folsom site in eastern New Mexico, where spear points were found embedded in the remains of an extinct bison, represents the first chapter of their long story. This story, as evidenced in Archaic campsites,

Mogollon pithouses, Anasazi pueblos, and Spanish missions, has continued over thousands of years; there is no end in sight to man's presence in the Southwest.

In an age such as our own, when the pace of external change often exceeds our ability to adapt, ancient ruins can have more than a purely scenic or romantic appeal. Ruins are time anchors, giving substance to an elusive past. They are also the headstones, if you will, of deceased cultures. Ruins memorialize the successes and failures of our predecessors and remind us of the mortality of civilization.

Accustomed as most Americans are to physical comfort and convenience, it is natural to regard prehistoric Indian society as having functioned at a very remote and alien level of primitiveness. So indeed it did. And yet, putting aside contrasting material inventories, we soon discover that many basic forces governing the development of ancient societies — climate, environment, natural resources — still remain of vital importance to our own well-being. Were the Sinagua of the upper Little Colorado River any more awed by the 1064 eruption of Sunset Crater than were Oregonians by events at Mount St. Helens almost a millenium later? Was the Anasazis' thirteenth-century search for firewood on the Mesa Verde any more or less urgent than our own exploration for fossil fuels? How do *they* and *we* compare as victims of drought, flood, famine, disease, or social disorder? Having an awareness of the continuing shared concerns of human beings over time and of repeated patterns of history only deepens and enlarges our appreciation of archaeological sites. With some understanding of prehistory, weather-worn petroglyphs and grassy pueblo mounds assume a certain vitality. As for the towers of Hovenweep or the ramparts of Wupatki, they take on an aspect of discarded theatrical sets from an age-old drama whose cast has changed but whose theme may once again be replayed.

Acknowledgments

I would like to thank the following people for their support and assistance during the preparation of this book: Philip W. Brittenham, James Bradford, T. J. Ferguson, George J. Gummerman, Karl Kernberger, Richard W. Lang, Ruth Meria-Noble, Dan Murphy, Matts Myhrman, Polly Schaafsma, Cherie Scheick, Douglas W. Schwartz, Jane Whitmore, and Arthur H. Wolf. I would also like to express my appreciation to The Amerind Foundation, the U.S. Bureau of Land Management, the Laboratory of Anthropology Library of the Museum of New Mexico, the Museum of Northern Arizona, the National Park Service, and the School of American Research for their support.

It goes almost without saying that a book such as this would never have been possible without the contributions of generations of archaeologists who have investigated southwestern ruins and without the efforts of many people and agencies responsible for the creation, maintenance, and safekeeping of these public archaeological preserves. Thanks to them, too.

ANCIENT RUINS
OF THE SOUTHWEST

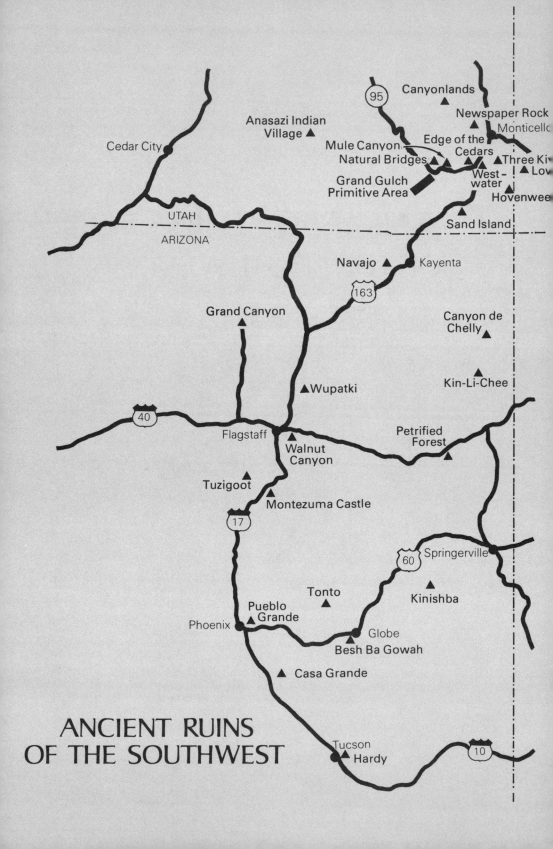

95

Canyonlands ▲

Anasazi Indian
Village ▲

Newspaper Rock
▲   Monticello

Mule Canyon   Edge of the
Natural Bridges   Cedars
▲   ▲ Three Ki▲
West-   ▲ Lo▲
water
▲
Hovenwee▲

Grand Gulch
Primitive Area

Cedar City ●

UTAH

ARIZONA

Sand Island
▲

Navajo ▲   Kayenta

163

Grand Canyon ▲

Canyon de
Chelly
▲

Kin-Li-Chee
▲

40

▲ Wupatki

Petrified
Forest
▲

Flagstaff
▲
Walnut
Canyon

Tuzigoot ▲

▲
Montezuma Castle

17

60   Springerville

Tonto
▲

Kinishba
▲

Pueblo
Grande
▲
Phoenix ●

Globe ●   Besh Ba Gowah

▲ Casa Grande

ANCIENT RUINS
OF THE SOUTHWEST

Tucson ●
▲ Hardy

10

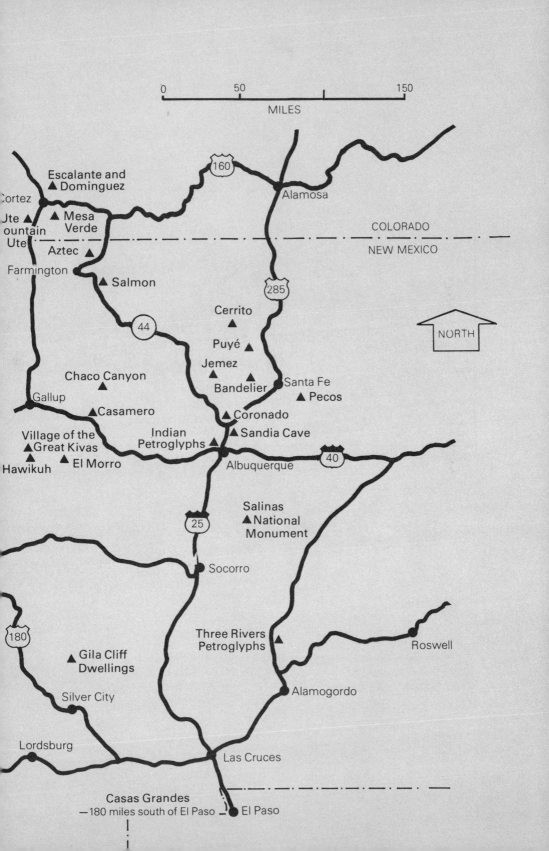

MILES

0   50   150

(160)

▲ Escalante and Dominguez

Cortez

Alamosa

COLORADO

NEW MEXICO

Ute ▲ Mountain Ute

▲ Mesa Verde

Aztec ▲

Farmington

(285)

▲ Salmon

Cerrito ▲

(44)

Puyé ▲

Jemez ▲

Chaco Canyon ▲

Bandelier ▲

Santa Fe

Gallup

▲ Casamero

▲ Coronado

▲ Pecos

Village of the ▲ Great Kivas

Indian Petroglyphs ▲

▲ Sandia Cave

NORTH

▲
Hawikuh   ▲ El Morro

Albuquerque

(40)

Salinas ▲ National Monument

(25)

Socorro

(180)

Three Rivers Petroglyphs ▲

Roswell

▲ Gila Cliff Dwellings

Silver City

Alamogordo

Lordsburg

Las Cruces

Casas Grandes
—180 miles south of El Paso

● El Paso

Mogollon pithouse reconstruction

THE MOGOLLON
Roots of Southwestern Culture

Southwestern Indian culture had its beginnings among a people of shadowy origins who disappeared long before Columbus set foot in the New World. Known as the Mogollon (mug-ee-yone), they were the first Southwesterners to cultivate corn, make pottery, and build pithouses in which to live. These important developments spread throughout the Southwest and reached a culmination after the eleventh century among a people called the Anasazi.

The early Mogollon were a mountain people who lived in small settlements along the high, wooded, well-watered country that descends in a curve from the upper tributaries of the Little Colorado River through the southern Arizona— New Mexico border country, and on further south beyond Casas Grandes in the Mexican state of Chihuahua. This long mountainous arc lay to the south of the plateaus inhabited by the Anasazi and to the north and east of the desert river valleys of another prehistoric group, the Hohokam. Due perhaps to the diverse geography of their territory, the Mogollon were never a cohesive society; rather, they consisted of scattered groups sharing many basic cultural traits but also expressing regional differences.

Preceding the Mogollon were a nomadic hunting and gathering people known in archaeological literature as the Cochise. Over a period of centuries, the Cochise gave up nomadism in favor of horticulture and sedentary village life. After the completion of this cultural transition, archaeologists refer to these same people as Mogollon. The main catalyst for change among these hunters and gatherers was the introduction of corn from Mexico where it had been under cultivation since at least 7000 B.C. While new and improved genetic strains of corn were introduced to the Southwest over time, local varieties became better adapted to cold and drought. In addition, the southwestern natives were attaining greater yields through more sophisticated horticultural methods. By around 300 B.C., the formerly nomadic Cochise had settled down to farming and village life, were building permanent habitations in the form of pithouses, and were making crude pottery.

Early Mogollon villages were small and usually situated on high ground. Later, probably for convenience, the people moved closer to their cultivated fields in the valleys. Mogollon pithouses were small round or oblong structures built over shallow excavations with low slab-lined walls and dirt floors that were pitted with storage cysts. Upright posts supported roof timbers that were often set in a conical formation and overlaid with sticks, grass, and a layer of dirt. Villages averaged fifteen or twenty houses and usually included one larger pithouse possibly used for religious ceremonies or other public functions.

Pottery in the New World was first developed in Mesoamerica, but knowledge of this craft was brought up to the Mogollon area around the same time as corn became domesticated. Although pottery was breakable and

Mimbres bowl depicting arrow makers. Collection of the School of American Research. Photograph by Fred Stimpson.

less portable than basketry, it had numerous advantages for a sedentary people. Pots were better suited for carrying water and cooking and more effective as storage vessels for seeds. As an archaeological artifact, pottery is of inestimable value. Potsherds, which are nonperishable, can be analyzed many centuries after being discarded to determine their approximate date and the cultural identity of their makers. Pottery also contains much common sense information about the activities of the people who used it.

From about A.D. 1000 to 1250, a branch of the Mogollon culture known as the Mimbres thrived in southwestern New Mexico. This group is well known today for the exquisitely decorated pottery it produced. Mimbres pots are off-white in color with black or dark brown painted designs, some geometric, others stylized representations of life forms including birds, animals, fish, and humans. Some Mimbres pottery images are narrative

and portray a fascinating view of the life and activities of these people. An unfortunate outgrowth of the beauty and desirability of Mimbres pottery has been the widespread looting of graves and outright destruction of sites by pothunters. Pothunting in southwestern New Mexico, in fact, has become a lucrative business and a serious threat to the preservation of a unique cultural and artistic heritage.

In its mountain environment, Mogollon culture dates from around 300 B.C. to A.D. 1350, although long before this latter date the Mogollon had become heavily influenced by Pueblo culture. After A.D. 1000, the construction of above-ground masonry structures, such as those found at Gila Cliffs, became favored over traditional pithouses. In other respects as well, Mogollon culture was infused with traits from the expansive and vigorous Anasazi of the Colorado Plateau. The Mogollon, however, were also influenced from the south, especially from the large population and trading center of Casas Grandes.

Readers may wonder why a prehistoric Indian group of such significance as the Mogollon are represented in the present guide by only three archaeological sites. This low monument profile is due largely to the fact that these early people built perishable dwellings in an area of substantial rainfall. To reconstruct a pithouse village would by no means be impossible, but public support for such an enterprise has not yet materialized and does not seem probable in the near future. One must recognize that deteriorated pithouses have an uphill road to tread in attracting the sort of public enthusiasm that the cliff dwellings of Mesa Verde or the five-storied pueblos of Chaco Canyon have so long enjoyed. Perhaps the days of Mogollon popularity has yet to come, however, and future decades will witness enthusiasts queued up to enter reconstructed pithouse villages in the southern New Mexico mountains as they do today at the dramatic Anasazi ruins of the Colorado Plateau.

Suggested reading: *Mogollon Culture Prior to A.D. 1000,* by Joe Ben Wheat. American Anthropological Association Memoir 82, Menasha, Wis., 1955.

Gila Cliff Dwellings National Monument

Gila Cliff Dwellings National Monument is located at the end of New Mexico 15, 44 miles from Silver City, New Mexico. This paved but winding road requires about two hours to drive. The monument also can be reached by New Mexico 35 through San Lorenzo and Mimbres. This route is easier driving.

These buildings occupy four caverns, the second of which toward the east is ten meters high. The western cave communicates with the others only from the outside, while the three eastern ones are separated by huge pillars, behind which are natural passageways from one cave to the other. The height of the floor above the bed of the creek is fifty-one meters, and the ascent is steep, in some places barely possible. To one coming from the mouth of the cleft, the caves become visible only after he passes them, so they are well concealed. But while it would be difficult for an Indian foe to take the place by storm, its inhabitants could easily be cut off from water or starved....

Among the many objects taken from these ruins, I mention particularly sandals made of strips of the yucca.... In addition, I saw many baskets or fragments of baskets; also prayer sticks and plume sticks. Such remains indicate that their makers were in no manner different from the Pueblo Indians in general culture.

Adolph F. Bandelier, 1884

Adolph Bandelier, the Southwest's pioneering anthropologist-explorer, was one of numerous early visitors to Gila (hee-la) Cliff Dwellings whose accounts mention collecting artifacts. How many other anonymous early settlers made excursions on horseback to the ruins and loaded their saddlebags? Probably many, for by the time archaeologists were able to study the cliff dwellings, little material culture remained with which to reconstruct their past.

The earliest ruin found in the monument, a Mogollon pithouse built in the open, dates from the first several centuries A.D. Mogollon culture thrived here until about A.D. 1000, when it became profoundly influenced by Pueblo culture from the north. This influence is particularly apparent in the architecture of Gila Cliff Dwellings but is also apparent in other elements of late

Above and right: Gila Cliff Dwellings

Mogollon material culture.

The ten or fifteen families who occupied Cliff Dwellers Canyon raised corn, beans, and squash on the mesas and cultivated gardens along portions of the stream beds. Like all prehistoric southwestern Indians, they also depended to a large extent on hunting game and gathering wild plants, and in addition, they traded actively with neighboring communities.

At Gila Cliffs, one can see forty masonry rooms built in the shelter of five deep caves 150 feet or more above the canyon floor. Despite early vandalism, the pueblo's walls are remarkably well preserved. Dates obtained from original roof timbers indicate that these dwellings were built in the 1280s. Abandonment of the site was complete by A.D. 1400.

Persons visiting Gila Cliff Dwellings should go first to the visitor center for information and a trail guide to the ruins. From the center, there is a mile and a half drive to the trailhead. The path crosses the West Fork of the Gila River, winds up Cliff Dwellers Canyon about half a mile, then loops back to the caves. In the shade of tall pines, this scenic walk initially follows the creek, then leads into some steeper climbing. One is able to enter all but one of the caves and walk among the cliff dwellings, where there are numerous opportunities for good photographs. From the ruins, the trail returns by a different route to the river and parking area. At least one hour should be planned for the tour.

Gila Cliff Dwellings National Monument encompasses only 533 acres but is surrounded by over three million acres of National Forest, one of the most beautiful and primitive regions of North America. A century ago, this country was the stronghold of Geronimo, the Apache guerrilla leader whose resistance to American settlement of the Southwest is a legend. Master of this rugged terrain, Geronimo was able to strike and withdraw at will, and for many years eluded capture by the American army. Today, the Gila Wilderness, with over two thousand miles of trails, is a

paradise for hikers, backpackers, and packtrippers. One can roam this area for weeks without meeting another soul.

A Forest Service campground is maintained near the monument, and gas, food, and camping supplies can be purchased at nearby Gila Hot Springs. Travel services of all kinds are available in Silver City.

Three Rivers Petroglyph Site

Three Rivers is an intersection along U.S. 54, 30 miles north of Alamogordo, New Mexico. To reach the petroglyph preserve, turn east at this intersection and proceed for 5 miles to the entrance to the site's parking lot. From here, one trail leads through the extensive petroglyph area and another leads to an archaeological excavation.

Rock art is found throughout the areas of the Southwest where prehistoric as well as more recent peoples have lived, traveled, hunted, drawn water, or performed religious ceremonies. The images, pecked or scratched into stone or painted on cliff and cave walls, often have survived in remarkably fine condition over many centuries. Rock art sites are widely scattered, often located on privately owned land, in remote canyons, or in areas where protection from vandalism has not been feasible. The sites are usually well known to archaeologists and local residents, but many are seen and appreciated only rarely by the general public. Except in reproduction, petroglyphs and rock paintings cannot be exhibited in museums and, traditionally, anthropologists have not considered this phenomenon a serious subject of in-

quiry. Until recently, few easily available publications on this interesting and sometimes inspiring art form have been available.

A petroglyph (Greek *petros,* a stone, and *glyphe,* carving) is an image that has been pecked, chiseled, grooved, or scratched into a rock surface. Petroglyphs were usually made by rubbing or striking a stone against the drawing surface. Sometimes, to achieve greater control, the chisel-stone was placed against the rock and then struck with a heavier hammer-stone. The end result was to wear away or knock off the darker oxidized exterior or patina, exposing a lighter undersurface. Petroglyphs vary greatly, from thinly scratched doodlings and scrawls, to more deeply etched stylized representations of the natural world, to carefully conceived designs.

The Three Rivers petroglyph site is one of two areas in New Mexico set aside solely because of its collection of rock art. Approximately five thousand pictures representing humans, animals, birds, fish, reptiles, insects, and plants, as well as a variety of geometric and abstract designs, are scattered over fifty acres of a long ridgetop near the western base of the Sacramento Mountains, in the central-southern portion of the state. These images were drawn by Jornada Mogollon people between A.D. 900 and 1400. It is speculated that the site lay along a well-traveled route, was a lookout area for game, or had religious significance. The artists probably lived in a village located a short distance south of the site that has been partly excavated and can be visited. The predecessors of the Mescalero Apaches, who live east of Three Rivers on a reservation, arrived in the Southwest long after these rock artists had gone.

Most of the Three Rivers petroglyphs are crude, sketchy, and hard to translate into familiar life forms. But scattered among the scribbled images

Petroglyph of mountain sheep, Three Rivers Petroglyph Site

are many pictures executed in a more accomplished and finished style. The petroglyphs appear grayish-white on the dark surface of boulders. A trail nearly a mile long winds along the ridge, passing many of the more interesting petroglyphs. Uncounted more can be found by digressing from the path.

Although the Three Rivers site is often hot and windy and one has to work to see much of the rock art, an excursion here is well worth the time and effort. One can sit among the boulders, surrounded by the spirit images of a long ago people, and reflect on the little known events this landscape must have witnessed. Were these rock artists doodling, expressing thoughts, recording events, speaking to their gods, practicing magic? And what became of them? The site offers little hard information, but questions

raised are often more interesting than answers given.

Archaeologists have identified several prehistoric settlements or villages in the vicinity, and an interpretive trail beginning at the east side of the parking lot leads to two recently excavated and partially reconstructed pueblo houses and a full size replica of a Mogollon pithouse from circa A.D. 1000. All who enter, however, should keep an eye out for rattlesnakes, which have been reported roosting among the ceiling timbers in hot weather.

At the parking lot, visitors will find picnic tables, barbecue pits, drinking water, and toilets. Trailers and pickup campers are welcome to park overnight. A National Forest Service campground is located several miles beyond the petroglyph turnoff, but the nearest travel services and overnight accommodations are in Alamogordo or Carrizozo. Other nearby places of interest include the Mescalero Apache reservation east of Tularosa, White Sands National Monument, and the historic town of Lincoln.

Suggested reading: *Rock Art of the American Indian,* by Campbell Grant. Thomas Y. Crowell Company, 1967. Apollo Edition, 1972.

Casas Grandes

The Casas Grandes site is located just outside the village of Casas Grandes, Chihuahua, Mexico, approximately 300 kilometers southwest of Ciudad Juarez on Mexico 2. Juarez is across the Rio Grande from El Paso, Texas.

Perhaps the most impressive prehistoric ruin in the Southwest is the Casas Grandes site located across the border in Mexico. In size, Casas Grandes, which is twenty-seven times larger than Chaco Canyon's Pueblo Bonito, is almost in a category of its own. And the levels of technological and commercial sophistication achieved by its inhabitants were unsurpassed by any indigenous community or group in the American Southwest.

Casas Grandes is located in northern Chihuahua in a broad valley that receives ten to twenty inches of rain annually plus the drainage from 18,000 square miles of surrounding mountains. The basin and range topography of this region extends unbroken into southern New Mexico and Arizona, and the Casas Grandes inhabitants maintained active cultural and economic links with groups from these northern areas. The varied local environment — desert flats to high mountains — was fully exploited and formed the

basis for a growing population and thriving trade center.

A large portion of the Casas Grandes site, including much of Paquimé, its core city, was excavated by the Amerind Foundation of Dragoon, Arizona, between 1958 and 1961. Subsequently, the archaeological findings of this large project have been published in a series of illustrated volumes including over one thousand pages of synthesis by Amerind Director, Charles C. Di Peso. While it would be impossible to summarize these reports in the present format, a few general observations will help inform readers what to expect at the site.

Village life in the Casas Grandes Valley began to develop around A.D. 700 when this region represented little more than the barbarous northern frontier of the progressive and civilized culture far to the south. But enterprising Mesoamerican entrepreneurs or *puchtecas* recognized the potential of Casas Grandes as a commercial base and moved up here to organize local support and begin construction of Paquimé. Under their leadership and expertise, Paquimé became the nucleus of an empire, with thousands of satellite or culturally associated villages, dominion over 85,000 square miles of land in northwestern Chihuahua and northeastern Sonora, and control over a trade network reaching hundreds of miles to the north. Dr. Di Peso likens the Casas Grandes system of commerce with that of the Hudson Bay Company in Canada, whose extensive network of traders and trading posts served to exchange materials (and ideas) across vast distances between culturally disparate societies. In the Casas Grandes case, however, prime trade items included parrot feathers and turquoise rather than furs.

The commercial success of Casas Grandes fed directly into the city itself as evidenced in its tremendous growth after circa A.D. 1060 and in the

The Casas Grandes site. Niches around plaza were turkey pens. Courtesy of The Amerind Foundation.

extensive urban renewal that took place in the mid-thirteenth century. Large marketplaces were built as well as warehousing facilities, ceremonial mounds, plazas, ball courts, and a complex of high-rise apartment buildings. Di Peso speculates that the dramatic architecture of Paquimé probably was planned in part to entice large numbers of visitors from the hinterlands to further "fill the larders of the city and its masters." No doubt such a strategy was successful, and as power focused on the city, it was probably possible to involve rural inhabitants in the construction of the extraordinary water control system.

This system began to the northwest of the city at Varelemo Warm Springs, which today produce over three thousand gallons of water per minute. This flow was brought to Paquimé in aqueducts and stored in a reservoir from which it was dispensed in underground stone-lined channels that serviced the main house clusters.

Drainage tunnels and large subterranean walk-in cisterns were other features of the system.

In addition to a domestic water system, Casas Grandes inhabitants enjoyed the benefits of heated sleeping platforms, airy living-room spaces, raised-platform cooking hearths, city parks, and what must have been an exciting marketplace complex. Some of the plazas were bordered by rows of turkey and macaw pens; aviculture is believed to have been a principal source of wealth and renown.

After 1261, the socio-political system of Casas Grandes began to come apart, and the city fell into increasing disrepair. Civil construction and public maintenance ceased, and the society suffered from a crippling economic depression. The situation seems to have been worsened by an earthquake and by a meteor strike; both probably had a devastating effect on public morale in addition to causing property damage. Enemy attack and/or a broad-based regional revolt are also cited as possible causes for the social disintegration and physical destruction of the city. Whatever the circumstances, by 1340 Casas Grandes had fallen, and the brilliant city of Paquimé was but a memory. When the first Europeans entered the area over two centuries later, they found the ancient city in ruins and the valley virtually abandoned.

Thanks to an arid climate, the massiveness of the buildings, and stabilization efforts by the Mexican government, the Casas Grandes site has not experienced heavy erosional damage since excavations were completed. Floor features, of course, have disappeared and the temple mounds are gullied, but the high adobe walls of former buildings still stand, and in visiting the ruins, one quickly recognizes that a powerful and superbly organized society was once seated here. In this sense, interesting comparisons can be made with the prehistoric complex of Chaco Canyon in New Mexico, which certainly had close ties with Casas Grandes in commerce, as well as to sites such as Casa Grande in southern Arizona.

If there is a disappointing aspect to visiting Casas Grandes, it lies in the absence of interpretive facilities or professional guides. Before coming here, one would benefit greatly by spending some time with the three Di Peso synthesis volumes on the site's archaeology.

Americans coming to this monument will be interested also in seeing the historic town of Casas Grandes located adjacent to the ruins. The rustic adobe buildings and plaza of this small community are reminiscent of numerous New Mexico towns as they probably looked in territorial days. Nuevo Casas Grandes, several kilometers from the site, has motels, restaurants, gas stations, and other travel facilities. The highways to Columbus, New Mexico, and El Paso, Texas, are well marked and in good condition.

Suggested reading: *Casas Grandes: A Fallen Trading Post of the Gran Chichimeca,* 3 vols. by Charles C. Di Peso. Northland Press, 1974.

THE HOHOKAM
Desert Farmers and Craftsmen

There has been much research, writing, and speculation on the Mesoamerican roots of prehistoric southwestern culture, and while scholars all agree on the importance of the northern spread of influences from the more ancient civilizations of southern Mexico, they have not as yet traced in detail what development came from what region, nor at what time. Although there are many gaps of knowledge and differences of opinion, there is little disagreement among scientists that the Hohokam, the principal prehistoric inhabitants of southern Arizona, played an active role in what has been called "the Mexican connection."

The Hohokam appeared along the Gila River in about the third century B.C. Although some archaeologists have seen this appearance as a local development out of the Cochise hunter-gatherer tradition, the prevailing belief today is that the Hohokam were immigrants from the south. No geographical area of origin, however, has been pinpointed. In its early phase, Hohokam culture closely resembled that of the Mogollon to the north and east; later, however, it exhibited an inventiveness, creativity, and energy that far surpassed its mountain-dwelling neighbors.

Anthropologists distinguish two basic groups of Hohokam: the Desert and the Riverine. The Desert Hohokam, smaller in population and less progressive in achievements, did not live near streams. Although they made serious efforts to utilize surface runoff, their agricultural accomplishments were minimal; they remained essentially gatherers and hunters. The Riverine Hohokam, on the other hand, established settlements along desert rivers and practiced water management to a degree unapproached by any other aboriginal North Americans. They became accomplished irrigation farmers and achieved the kind of food surplus and specialization to allow the production of elaborate craftwork and the development of far-reaching trade contacts. During the period following their arrival in the American Southwest, Hohokam territory was limited to the region around present-day Phoenix. Gradually their population grew and their territory expanded east up the Gila River, south down the Santa Cruz beyond Tucson, and north up the Verde River Valley and even as far as the Flagstaff area. Their influence, especially as farmers and craftsmen, touched every Indian group with which they had contact.

The extensive irrigation canals of the Hohokam, begun eighteen centuries before the discovery of America, would be praiseworthy even by contemporary standards. Considering the crude hand tools available one thousand to two thousand years ago, the Hohokam canals represent a truly extraordinary accomplishment. This canal system reached its height between A.D. 1000 and 1400, the period of the Hohokam's greatest strength as a culture. One village, Los Muertos, excavated in 1887–88 by Frank H. Cushing, was served by a single six-mile canal from the Salt River. It is apparent that in addition to making

Archaeologist Emil Haury in excavated Snaketown canal. Courtesy of the Arizona State Museum. Photograph by Helga Teiwes.

farming possible in the desert, canals also offered the Hohokam a degree of flexibility in selecting village sites. The labor required in canal digging required untold man-hours, and since canals often served more than one village, smoothly administered intercommunity cooperation was needed to maintain and operate the system. All these factors required a strong, well-ordered, and well-disciplined society.

Corn, beans, and squash comprised the nutritional base of the Hohokam, but this was supplemented by food collecting in the desert environment they knew so well. Many varieties of plants were gathered for their fruit, juice, nuts, seeds, bulbs, and fiber. A staple such as the saguaro, a giant

cactus that stands sentinel-like in the southern Arizona deserts, contained a wealth of riches. Its fruit was eaten and its juice fermented to wine and vinegar. The latter was used to etch shell in the making of jewelry, a technique perfected by the Hohokam four hundred years prior to its practice in Europe. In addition, saguaro ribs were used as a building material and saguaro seeds to tan hides. Two facts are helpful to remember in considering the long success of Hohokam culture. First, this arid region was and is naturally productive of many plants supportive of human life that are not utilized by modern society. And second, the Gila River was prehistorically a much more constant and

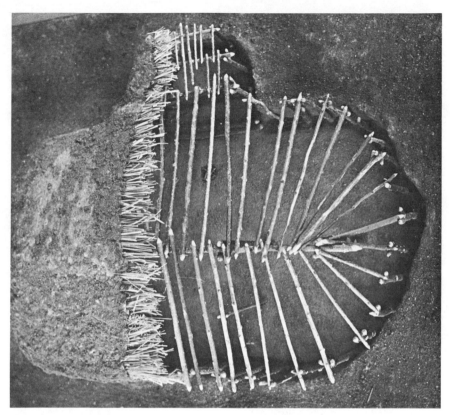

Cut-away model of Hohokam house on display at Montezuma Well

dependable source of water than it is today. As recently as one hundred years ago, the Gila supported fish and shellfish and provided havens for game and waterfowl. Its diminished and erratic flow today is a consequence of relatively recent heavy logging activities in the mountains, of irrigation, and of other human activities relating to the fast growing metropolitan area of Phoenix.

Hohokam villages, for the most part, were less striking visually than the masonry cliff houses and pueblos of the Anasazi. Apparently built without concern for defense, the houses were scattered, seemingly at random, over a large area. Snaketown, south of Phoenix, which saw fourteen hundred

years of Hohokam occupation, covers at least one square-kilometer. As for the dwellings themselves, they were modified pithouses — shallow excavations in the ground, roofed over by sticks, reeds, and mud. The villages also contained trash mounds that grew to considerable size over the centuries and were used as platforms for ceremonial purposes. In its later period, Hohokam architecture was much influenced by Pueblo culture to the north and also by Salado culture in the Tonto Basin. This influence is apparent at such sites as Pueblo Grande and Casa Grande.

To the disappointment of archaeologists, the Hohokam cremated their dead in pits that contain little more than ashes and broken bits and pieces of artifacts. The absence of skeletons has denied scientists the opportunity of comparing Hohokam physical features with those of other cultural groups who may represent their progenitors or descendants.

An outstanding achievement of the Hohokam, much appreciated today by lay people as well as by archaeologists and art historians, was their jewelry. Indeed, they were masters of this craft, particularly in the working of shell, which they imported from the Gulf of California. Hohokam decorative objects include beads, pendants, bracelets, rings, necklaces, hairpins, and nose, ear, and lip plugs. Their carving, etching, mosaic overlay, stone sculpture, ceramic figurines, and pottery designs all identify the Hohokam as outstanding craftspeople whose products made an enduring contribution to native southwestern culture and its history.

Nearly one hundred Hohokam ball courts are known. This fact in itself suggests the significance of this ritual game that undoubtedly was derived from the Maya and Toltec cultures of southern Mexico. Ball courts date as early as A.D. 700 and were in use until 1400. In addition to whatever ritual, religious, and recreational significance they held, the ball courts represent the Hohokams' most outstanding architectural achievement. Semicircular in form, they were made by excavating a playing field (185 by 63 feet at Snaketown) around which high massive earthen banks were built. Three stones were placed as markers, two at the center ends of the court and one in the middle. Only one rubber ball, buried in a ceramic jar near Casa Grande, has been found.

The Hohokam, who appeared around 300 B.C. and vanished in about A.D. 1400, represent a seminal southwestern culture. They were expert farmers, water engineers, craftsmen, and traders. Their culture, which probably grew from Mesoamerican roots

and continued to receive stimulus from this source, developed its own strong identity and made significant engineering, agricultural, and artistic strides. *Hohokam* is a Piman word meaning "those who have gone" or who have "been all used up," and it is generally believed by Indian and anthropologist alike that the Hohokam were the direct ancestors of present-day Pima and Papago Indians. Considerable evidence, both archaeological and ethnographic, points to this conclusion. If this is in fact true, between the early fifteenth century, when Hohokam sites were last occupied, and the sixteenth and seventeenth centuries, when Europeans arrived and described the Pimas and Papagos, the culture experienced a dramatic and as yet unexplained decline.

Suggested reading: *The Hohokam: Desert Farmers and Craftsmen, Excavations at Snaketown, 1964 – 1965,* by Emil W. Haury. The University of Arizona Press, Tucson, Arizona, 1976.

Casa Grande Ruins National Monument

Casa Grande Ruins National Monument is located on State Highway 87 1 mile north of Coolidge, Arizona. This is almost midway between Phoenix and Tucson.

In November, 1694, I went inland with my servants and some justices of this Pimeria, as far as the casa grande, as these Pimas call it, which is on the large River of Hila that flows out of Nuevo Mexico.... The casa grande is a four-story building as large as a castle and equal to the largest church in these lands of Sonora.... Close to this casa

18

Casa Grande ruins

grande there are thirteen smaller houses, somewhat more dilapidated, and the ruins of many others, which makes it evident that in ancient times there had been a city here.

Eusebio Kino, 1694

The best preserved ruins are built of stone or lie in protective caves. If this is an archaeological rule, then its exception is a massive, multistoried adobe house that has stood on an open plain, exposed to sun, wind, rain, and varying desert temperatures for over five hundred years. Its very existence today as more than just a dirt mound on the flat landscape testifies to the unusual architectural and en-

gineering skills of its fourteenth-century builders.

Casa Grande is a ruin that has long perplexed archaeologists. What was it? A variety of speculations on its original function, some based on serious research, have included a large residence, a storage house, a temple or palace, an administrative center, and an observatory for stargazers.

The occupants of Casa Grande were Hohokam, who moved into the Gila Valley around 300 B.C. and developed an extensive system of irrigation agriculture. From its uppermost story, a view is attained of the lower section of Casa Grande's main canal, whose intake was sixteen miles upriver. During all but the last century of their long

Artist's reconstruction of Casa Grande. Courtesy of the National Park Service.

history, the Hohokam lived in small perishable mud and stick huts. But in the twelfth century, Pueblo-style house construction made an appearance in the desert and mountain regions of central southern Arizona. This type of building may have been introduced through the Salado people who were centered in the Tonto Basin to the north. Casa Grande represents the peak of Hohokam-Pueblo architecture and village planning.

The Hohokam, including the people of Casa Grande, disappeared as a culture by the mid-fifteenth century. What happened to them is not known. One reasonable speculation points to crop failure resulting from waterlogging and salinization of agricultural land from long intensive irrigation. Another theory suggests that perhaps the irrigation system itself broke down as a consequence of lateral erosion by the river, which cut out canal heads. Whatever the cause, by 1450 the Hohokam were gone, leaving Casa Grande to be victimized by the

natural elements for more than two centuries before discovery by Spanish explorers.

Casa Grande's most immediate interest is as a building. It was built principally of caliche earth, a desert subsoil with high lime content. Wood found in the site included ponderosa pine, white fir, juniper, and mesquite. Some of this material had to have been transported from mountain regions more than fifty miles distant. There were over six hundred roof beams, and over fifteen hundred cubic yards of soil were used in wall construction. These data give an idea of the amount of labor involved in the building of this structure.

The walls of Casa Grande are deeply trenched in the ground. At their base, they are four and a half feet thick tapering to two feet at full height. The mud was mixed in depressions to a thick consistency, carried to the walls, and puddled by hand in courses of about twenty-six inches. Evidence of these courses is clearly visible today in wall-cracking. The basic house was only two stories high, but the first story was set on five feet of fill to give the house greater height and presumably better visibility over the surrounding countryside. A single third story room was added that had holes in one wall that line up precisely with sunset at the equinoxes. It is this peculiarity that lends credence to the theory of the house functioning at least in part as a celestial observatory.

One hundred and fifty-four years passed following the initial Spanish penetration into the Southwest before the first European laid eyes on Casa Grande. In 1694, a Jesuit missionary by the name of Eusebio Francisco Kino, guided by Sobaipuri Indians, came down the Santa Cruz River and recorded the existence of the ruin. It became a natural landmark for subsequent exploratory expeditions as well as for later travelers, frontiersmen, soldiers, settlers, and tourists. By 1880, the Southern Pacific Railroad had a station only twenty miles away and visitation increased markedly. At this time, the ruins had virtually no more protection from souvenir hunters and vandals than it did from the weather. National interest in protecting the site began to crystallize following the 1887–88 Henenway Southwestern Archaeological Expedition, which included such illustrious scientific names as Frank H. Cushing, J. Walter Fewkes, Adolph F. Bandelier, and Frederick Webb Hodge. In 1892, 480 acres were set aside for the protection of the ruin. The first roof over the site was built eleven years later. Between 1906 and 1908, archaeological excavations and drainage and stabilization work were conducted by Fewkes, and in 1918, Casa Grande achieved status as a national monument.

Today the monument includes a picnic area, a small desert botanical garden, and an interpretive museum. Included in the latter are displays of Hohokam ceramics, tools, and jewelry, a chart depicting the prehistoric canal system, and various other cultural exhibits. Interpretive talks are sometimes given by rangers and a printed trail guide is available. Although gardens, museum, and ruins can be seen in less than an hour, many people will certainly want to spend a somewhat longer time seeing this monument. Food, lodging, and other travel services are available in Coolidge, Florence, and other nearby towns. Several public campgrounds are located in the vicinity, though not at the monument itself.

Suggested reading: *The Architecture of the Casa Grande and Its Interpretation,* by David R. Wilcox and Lynette O. Shenk. Archaeological Series No. 115, Arizona State Museum, 1977.

The Hardy Site

The Hardy Site is located in Fort Lowell Park at 2900 North Craycroft Road, in Tucson, Arizona.

First reported in 1884 by Adolph Bandelier, the Hardy Site contains the remains of a large Hohokam village that once covered about one-fourth of a square mile. This site was occupied from about A.D. 300 to 1250. The Hohokam of the Tucson Basin were related culturally to other Hohokam communities further north along the Gila and Salt Rivers. They were farmers who raised crops along desert streams and used the nearby mountains for hunting and gathering edible plants and seeds.

A small portion of the Hardy Site was excavated in the late 1970s by the Arizona State Museum. Found in these excavations were clusters of pithouses, trash mounds, outside roasting pits, caliche mining pits, work areas, and a cemetery and offertory plaza. Afterwards, the excavations were backfilled with dirt. At the site, a pithouse floor was reconstructed out of cement, duplicating the appearance of the original floor. In addition, ten panels depicting various aspects of Hohokam life and culture were erected. There are no ruins to be viewed at the Hardy Site. Hohokam houses were usually built of sticks, grass, and mud and deteriorated soon after abandonment. Casa Grande and Pueblo Grande were the products of late Hohokam history when Pueblo-style architecture had penetrated to southern Arizona. There is some possibility of forming a national monument of Snaketown, a large village with a long history located south of Phoenix along the Gila River. If this happens, hopefully an effort will be made to reconstruct typical Hohokam stick and mud houses.

Fort Lowell, in Tucson, was built in the middle of the Hardy Site and the current display relating to the site is situated in Fort Lowell Park. An exhibit case containing Hardy artifacts and a diagram interpreting the site's chronology is located at nearby Fort Lowell Museum, which is open from 10:00 A.M. to 4:00 P.M. Wednesday through Saturday.

Pueblo Grande Ruins

The Pueblo Grande Museum and Ruins are located at 4619 East Washington Street in Phoenix, Arizona. From Interstate 10, take either the 48th Street or 40th Street exit going north.

The Salt River rises in the White Mountains of east central Arizona, flows into Roosevelt Reservoir in the Tonto Basin, and descends to the broad agricultural flatlands around Phoenix. Less than a mile from the Salt, on the east side of Phoenix, lies the partially excavated Hohokam village of Pueblo Grande. It is one of more than twenty large Hohokam archaeological sites located along an extensive prehistoric canal network in the Salt River Valley. Pueblo Grande itself is situated in the middle of an industrial-commercial district of east Phoenix. The popularity of this area for human habitation, it appears, has only increased with the passage of time.

The pueblo, constructed of mud and stone masonry, sits on an earthen platform, a practice once common fifteen hundred miles south in Mexico, but unusual in the American Southwest. The mound was retained by a massive wall consisting of chunks of caliche and river rocks. The pueblo's elevated position certainly must have provided its occupants with an advantageous visual perspective over the surrounding area and would have served well in event of attack. A second perimeter wall had been built around the pueblo itself, forming a compound that also would have been useful for defense.

Archaeological research at Pueblo Grande has been on-going for a number of years. It is thought the pueblo was built in the late 1100s by Hohokam people and that it experienced an influx of Salado people from the Tonto Basin after A.D. 1300. The Salado left after about a hundred years probably because of a rising water table resulting from long intensive irrigation and causing fields to become waterlogged.

Pueblo Grande today is skirted on two sides by modern canals, the lifeblood of the area's current booming prosperity. Barely visible in the distance, however, lie two Hohokam canals from the late twelfth or early thirteenth century. Although they are filled in and only visible by ridge lines

Pueblo Grande ruins

above their former banks, they once measured approximately twenty to thirty-three feet in width and ten to fourteen feet in depth. One was lined with clay to diminish water percolation through the underlying coarse gravel.

Pueblo Grande is entered through the Pueblo Grande Museum, which is adjacent to the site. This is a Phoenix municipal institution with exhibits relating to historic and prehistoric Indian occupation of southern Arizona. Its hours are 9:00 A.M. to 4:45 P.M. Mondays through Saturdays, and 1:00 P.M. to 4:45 P.M. on Sundays. An interpretive trail from the museum through the

ruins explains architectural features and excavation procedures and points out the canals and a ball court that lies about four hundred feet from the pueblo. Excavation of the court, which measures forty-one by eighty-five feet, involved the removal of an estimated fourteen thousand cubic feet of earth fill.

Pueblo Grande does not have the visual impact of many other southwestern archaeological sites, but it is one of only a very few ruins that relate to Hohokam culture and in combination with the adjoining museum makes for an interesting visit.

23

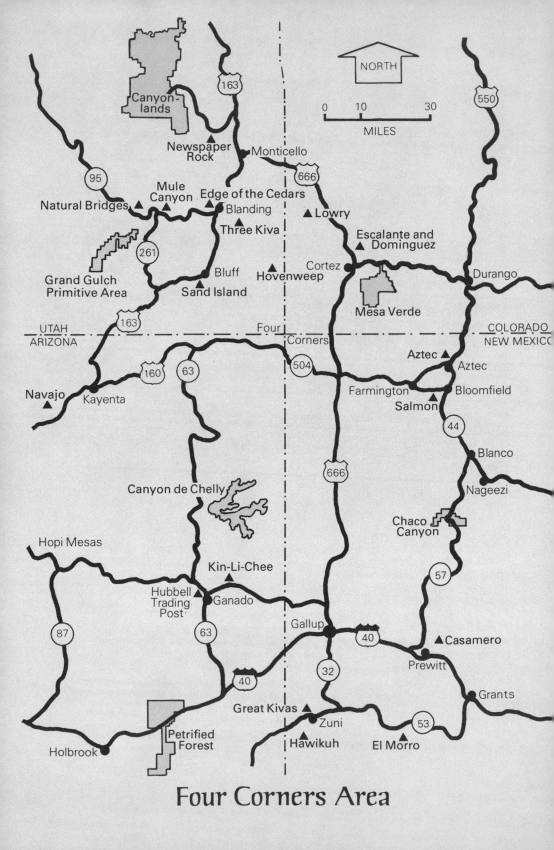

Four Corners Area

THE ANASAZI
From Prehistory to the Present

The prehistory of the North American Southwest is dominated by one vital, productive, and enduring culture—the Anasazi. This group of people emerged in the first several centuries B.C. out of a seminomadic hunting and gathering tradition to develop a settled village life with considerable dependence on horticulture. The first Anasazi were sheltered from the harsh winters of the Colorado Plateau by crude, shallow, one-family pithouses often built at the mouth of caves or under rock overhangs. Much later, the Anasazi acquired architectural and engineering skills that allowed them to build large multistoried masonry pueblos, and some have endured in remarkably fine condition to the present day.

The Navajo term *Anasazi,* translated loosely as "ancient ones," carries the connotation of a people who lived long ago and are no more. But despite the existence of centuries-old ruins from this culture, the Anasazi do not quite qualify as either a vanished race or a lost civilization. Both as a people and to some degree as a culture, they endured to become the Pueblo Indians who inhabit New Mexico and Arizona. Anyone attending a Hopi Bean Dance, Zuni Shalako ceremony, or feast day at Jemez will witness the spirit and world view of the Anasazi, nurtured over a hundred generations to manifest itself in a contemporary tradition.

The Anasazi story, still far from complete, has been compiled over the past century by an impressive array of anthropologists. This work began with such pioneers as Richard Weatherill and Adolph F. Bandelier, continued through the careers of Earl Morris, Alfred V. Kidder and others, and is carried on today by a host of distinguished archaeologists around the country. In a hundred years, the tools of this trade have evolved from pick and shovel to remote sensing photographic film and computers. The Anasazi have been investigated, analyzed, and reported on from nearly every conceivable angle by some five generations of scientists; and yet, any perusal of the literature will quickly reveal that many important questions still have no firm answers.

From around 7000 to 200 B.C., the Southwest was inhabited by small scattered bands of peoples who moved frequently as they hunted small game and collected edible plants, seeds, nuts, and fruit. Over many centuries, these hunter-gatherers acquired an increasing understanding of and control over the plants they used. In addition, from their Mogollon neighbors to the south, they obtained seeds from an all-important domestic Mesoamerican plant—corn. By the first few centuries B.C., these pre-Anasazi people found it increasingly advantageous to abandon their seminomadic lifestyle in favor of a more sedentary, communal existence revolving around the cultivation of corn, with beans and squash soon to be added to the gardens. This turn toward village life and farming is essentially what marks the birth of Anasazi culture about 2,200 years ago.

In discussing the Anasazi over this long span, archaeologists have for

ANASAZI CULTURAL/CHRONOLOGICAL CHART

Date	Pecos Classfication	Robert's Classification	Characteristics and Events
200 B.C.–A.D.450	Basketmaker I Basketmaker II	Basketmaker	Hunters and gatherers turning to horticulture. Habitations in caves. Atlatl in use. No pottery. Basketry.
450–700	Basketmaker III	Modified Basketmaker	Pithouse villages. Pottery made. Bow and arrow in use.
700–900 900–1100	Pueblo I Pueblo II	Developmental Pueblo	Above-ground pueblos. Pithouse becomes kiva. Cotton in use.
1100–1300	Pueblo III	Great Pueblo	Population expansion in uplands. Advances in agriculture, architecture, crafts. Developed complex socio-religious organization. Cliff dwellings.
1300–1700	Pueblo IV	Regressive Pueblo	Resettlement in new areas. Social and economic change.
1700–present	Pueblo V	Historic Pueblo	Strong influence from European culture. Much social, cultural, economic change. Some traditions continue.

convenience defined a sequence of developmental stages. In fact, unable to agree on a single classification system, several have been articulated over the years by different scholars. To the extent that reference is made to these systems of classification in museum exhibits, trail guides, and popular literature, the Anasazi Cultural/Chronological Chart shown above may prove useful.

The earliest Anasazi are known as Basketmakers as a result of the great number of finely woven baskets found by archaeologists in their burials. Later, some of the functions of baskets were taken over by pottery, and the Basketmakers, who lived in pithouses, began building above-ground masonry houses or *pueblos.* At this point, anthropologists drop the term Basketmaker in favor of Pueblo. Both terms, however, refer to the Anasazi culture at earlier and later stages of development and in many areas, pithouse and pueblo continued

contemporaneously for long periods.

As Anasazi culture progressed with a growing inventory of tools and utensils and better farming methods, population increased and settlements expanded over a larger territory. Elaborate ceremonialism replaced formerly simple religious rites, and social organization grew more complex. Trade networks covered most of the Southwest and extended to southern Mexico and the Gulf of California. Productivity in agriculture, craft manufacture, and building reached a peak between the mid-eleventh and mid-thirteenth centuries, the Great Pueblo period. Large population centers developed along the San Juan River and its tributaries, and elements of Pueblo culture spread widely throughout the Southwest region. The bust that followed this boom began after the

Right: Petroglyphs of macaw and macaw in cage, evidence of prehistoric trade with Mesoamerica, Indian Petroglyphs State Park

mid-1200s when Anasazi society began to suffer from an accumulation of problems. One of these, overuse of the environment and depletion of resources, was the logical consequence of large populations living in the same areas over a long period of time. People had to travel greater and greater distances for building materials and firewood and large game grew scarce. Communities were expending more physical energy and obtaining less in return. It is believed by some researchers that the thirteenth century witnessed a shift in the pattern of precipitation from winter snows and gentle spring rains to heavy summer thunderstorms that caused soil erosion and arroyo cutting. This climatic factor would have had a damaging effect on agriculture, the Pueblo economic and nutritional base. In some areas, notably Chaco Canyon and its satellites, it is possible that collapsing trade networks caused an economic depression. From 1276 to 1299, a serious drought occurred that further eroded an already fragile economy and caused the abandonment of the traditional Anasazi San Juan heartland. Refugees migrated south and east, to the area of the Hopi Mesas, the Zuni Mountains, the Little Colorado, and to the Rio Grande Valley.

It has been suggested that by the mid-1500s, Pueblo culture was experiencing a resurgence that might have brought it beyond its twelfth-century florescence. The Hopi, Zuni, and Rio Grande peoples were thriving, perhaps to a greater extent than their predecessors at Mesa Verde and Chaco Canyon. But in 1540, when Coronado stormed the Zuni pueblo of Hawikuh, an era began that profoundly altered the course of Pueblo development. In the early 1600s, Pueblo Indians saw the introduction of guns, foreign diseases, a dominant Spanish military, civil and ecclesiastical authority, a new religion, draft animals, and revolutionary farming techniques.

Over their long history, the Anasazi achieved remarkable success in many areas. They especially excelled as craftsmen, with pottery probably their most admired creation. Pueblo ceramics from the prehistoric era through today are gracefully and beautifully designed and hold a secure place in the realm of ethnic art. The full inventory of Anasazi crafts is a book length subject, but the following few examples will suggest the variety of craft skills practiced by these people: cord and plaited sandals; woven bowls, backpacks, water jugs; string nets and snares; woven mats; cotton fabrics; fur and feather blankets; shell, bead, and turquoise jewelry; bows and arrows; wooden combs; bone awls; whistles and flutes; ceramic and stone pipes; stone hoes, axes, hammers, and knives. Many of these items contain a degree of artistry that must have made them sought-after trade items.

Architecture is certainly the most monumental element of Anasazi culture and the aspect with which present readers will be most familiar. The three principal building materials were sandstone, adobe, and wood, but added to these was a knowledge of how to use natural landscape configurations to best practical and aesthetic advantage. The principles of Pueblo architecture are being incorporated into much building in the Southwest today. Some of the finest examples of Anasazi architecture are to be found in the finely constructed multi-storied pueblos of Chaco Canyon and the cliff dwellings of Mesa Verde.

The *kiva,* a Hopi term for ceremonial chamber, usually circular and subterranean, is a common feature at most Anasazi sites. Great kivas, typical of communities associated with Chaco Canyon, were larger expressions of the same type of structure and are believed to have served a larger community rather than a single pueblo or clan, and to have also functioned as centers for trade or social activities. The great

Back wall of Chettro Kettle, Chaco Canyon National Monument

kiva at Casa Rinconada in Chaco Canyon measures sixty-four feet in diameter and includes a series of antechambers and other peripheral rooms, two stairways, wall crypts, and a subfloor passageway. Kivas were an architectural holdover from Basketmaker pithouses and were usually entered by a hole in the roof that served also as an escape for hearth smoke. Climbing down the smokehole ladder was a purification ritual for participants in kiva ceremonies. Fresh air was drawn into a kiva by means of a ventilator shaft in the wall, the draft being deflected by a low wall or upright stone slab for better circulation. A small hole in the floor behind the hearth, called a *sipapu,* was a symbolic entrance to the underworld from which the Anasazi believed they once emerged. Other common kiva features are wall niches used for keeping ceremonial objects, foot drums, and wall benches.

Kivas, often inadequately described as a combination church and clubhouse, have no equivalent in the buildings of Western religions. As the center of ceremonial life in the pueblo, they were sacred places. They are believed to have been the domain of men who, in addition to carrying out religious activities, also used them for social interaction and for weaving. The pueblos of New Mexico and Arizona still have an active traditional religious life, and on ceremonial occasions, visitors will see dancers entering and exiting from kivas between plaza dances. Kivas represent what is probably the strongest physical link between contemporary Pueblo Indians and their most ancient Anasazi ancestors.

Suggested reading: *Anasazi: Ancient People of the Rock,* by Donald G. Pike. American West Publishing Company, Palo Alto, California, 1974. *The Anasazi,* by J. Richard Ambler. Museum of Northern Arizona, 1977.

29

Mesa Verde
National Park

The entrance to Mesa Verde National Park is located along U.S. 160 midway between Cortez and Mancos, Colorado, and 34 miles west of Durango. It is 21 miles of slow driving from the entrance to the park's headquarters and museum.

Far up above me, a thousand feet or so, set in a great cavern in the face of the cliff, I saw a little city of stone asleep. It was as still as sculpture—and something like that. It all hung together, seemed to have a kind of composition: pale little houses of stone nestling close to one another, perched on top of each other, with flat roofs, narrow windows, straight walls, and in the middle of the group, a round tower....

In sunlight it was the colour of winter oak leaves. A fringe of cedars grew along the edge of the cavern, like a garden. They were the only living things. Such silence and stillness and repose —immortal repose. That village sat looking down into the canyon with the calmness of eternity.... I had come upon the city of some extinct civilization, hidden away in this inaccessible mesa for centuries, preserved in the dry air and almost perpetual sunlight like a fly in amber, guarded by the cliffs and the river and the desert.

Willa Cather
The Professor's House

Mesa Verde has been called the Disneyland of American archaeology. Its many cliff dwellings set in great open caves create a feeling of fantasy and romance that seem more the creation of a Hollywood set designer than the remains of seven hundred-year-old Anasazi villages.

Left: Kiva, Kuaua ruins, Coronado State Park

To Richard Wetherill, the Mancos rancher who "discovered" these ruins, Mesa Verde was a rough wilderness in which no sensible cowboy would want to lose his cattle. But today the mesa is tamed and streams of summer tourists from around the world park at scenic overlooks, follow paved walks to cliff dwellings, and enjoy the conveniences of a modern resort. From a remote, almost forbidding area, where underbrush, cliffs, and labyrinthine canyons made travel difficult, Mesa Verde has become the most popular and accessible archaeological preserve in North America. Wetherill, after exploring and digging these ruins, dedicated much of his life to searching out the remains of Anasazi culture and was long frustrated by the apathetic public and scientific response to his discoveries. Were he alive today, he would no doubt be amazed and probably gratified to see the overwhelming attention that modern generations bestow upon his beloved ruins.

Mesa Verde's earliest recorded site dates to A.D. 608, relatively late considering that within a distance of fifty miles, Basketmaker sites have been found that are eight hundred years older. From the seventh through the twelfth centuries, most Mesa Verdeans resided in mesa-top pueblos, with few actually living in the caves. Only in the last hundred years of their occupation of the area did they build and live in the large cliff dwellings— Cliff Palace, Spruce Tree House, Balcony House, Long House, and others. Why were these mesas and canyons a good place to live? Answers are best found by looking at the natural environment.

The climate at Mesa Verde during its prehistoric occupation was similar to the conditions found today. Annual precipitation averaged eighteen inches, and with temperatures noticeably warmer than in the Mancos Valley below, the growing season was long enough to raise corn. Topsoil here consisted largely of

windblown silt from desert areas to the west and was suitable for raising crops. Natural resources useful to these Anasazi settlers included a variety of nutritious and medicinal plants, large trees such as Douglas fir, abundant game, reliable springs, and materials necessary for the manufacture of tools, pottery, basketry, and the construction of homes. The many habitable caves and rock shelters were almost a bonus.

Archaeologists do not know why many Mesa Verde people moved down to the canyons in the 1200s and built large cliff dwellings. Defense against invaders, notably nomadic Athapascans, has been a traditional explanation, but has few advocates today. It should be noted that while consolidation into pueblos of one hundred to two hundred rooms was the order of the day, most Mesa Verde Anasazi in the thirteenth century continued to live in small pueblos of ten to fifteen rooms and one kiva.

Recent surveys indicate that small numbers of Mesa Verde's population began to trickle away as early as the mid-eleventh century, and this gradual flow continued until the great exodus of the final decades of the thirteenth century. The causes of abandonment have been a key concern to archaeologists. Some interesting clues pointing to man-induced environmental depletion have emerged from studying the botanical and animal remains at Mesa Verde sites.

Douglas fir, a native of the area providing clean straight timbers, accounted for thirty percent of the beams used for house construction early in Mesa Verde's occupation. Prior to abandonment, this figure had dropped to three percent. This indication of deforestation is reinforced by another finding: in the eighth century, cottontails, a brush and woodland rabbit, were common, but five

Left: Cliff Palace,
Mesa Verde National Park

hundred years later had been replaced by jackrabbits, which thrive in open prairie. On the nutritional side, archaeological research has shown that consumption of bison, bighorn sheep, and mule deer by the early Mesa Verde inhabitants gradually switched to a dependence on rabbit, squirrel, and domestic turkey for meat. These and other data show that over centuries of use, Mesa Verde's environment became seriously depleted, with increasing scarcities of many resources essential in maintaining a large and healthy population. In such conditions, a drought such as occurred in the late 1200s would easily have brought on an exodus of the type that occurred in the final decades of the thirteenth century. Except for occasional use by Ute Indians, the mesa remained essentially abandoned until the late nineteenth century.

Few areas of the Southwest have enjoyed as much archaeological attention as Mesa Verde. National enthusiasm for these spectacular ruins account for much of the support generated to pay for costly excavations and ruins stabilization projects. The first excavators were Richard Wetherill and his brothers from Mancos. Wetherill was an interesting and controversial character who was fervently interested in the region's prehistoric heritage. He had an innate aptitude for archaeology but no scientific education or training in excavation methods. He was reportedly somewhat taken aback when, after shoveling out numerous ruins in what archaeologists today would consider record time, a visitor tactfully demonstrated the superiority of the trowel as an archaeological tool. Because of his lack of expertise and his proclivity for selling off vast quantities of artifacts, Wetherill's detractors regard him as a plunderer and profiteer; others, however, recognizing that he had to make a living and that nobody in the 1880s

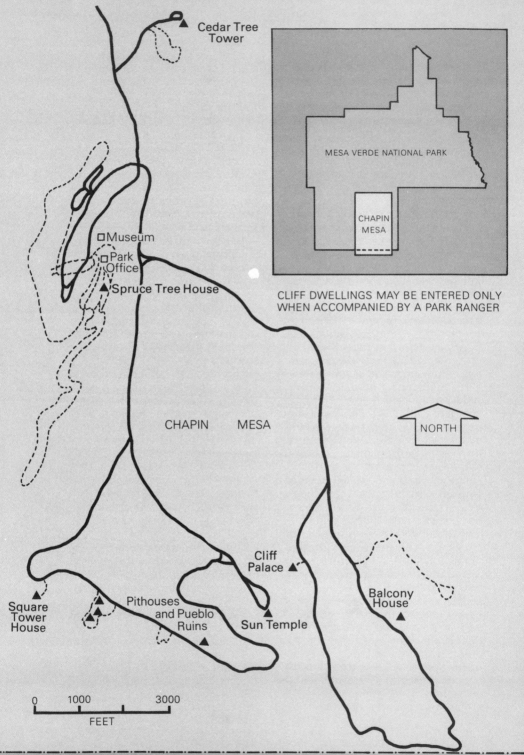

Cedar Tree Tower

MESA VERDE NATIONAL PARK

CHAPIN MESA

Museum

Park Office

Spruce Tree House

CLIFF DWELLINGS MAY BE ENTERED ONLY
WHEN ACCOMPANIED BY A PARK RANGER

NORTH

CHAPIN   MESA

Cliff Palace

Balcony House

Square Tower House

Pithouses and Pueblo Ruins

Sun Temple

0   1000   3000
FEET

UTE MOUNTAIN INDIAN RESERVATION

Mesa Verde National Park

knew much about digging ruins, judge him more generously. Since Wetherill's time, at least four generations of archaeologists have worked at Mesa Verde with results that would easily fill a bookshelf or museum. Following in the Wetherill tradition, two very distinguished Mesa Verde archaeologists, J. A. Lancaster and Alden Hayes, originally were ranchers.

Perhaps the first step in seeing Mesa Verde National Park is to stop at the Far View visitor center or Chapin Mesa park headquarters and museum for information about particular ruins and trails that are open and to find out when guided tours are scheduled. Some background information can also be obtained here on the natural and cultural histories of the area. In addition, the Chapin Mesa archaeological museum has an outstanding collection of Mesa Verde artifacts as well as a series of dioramas illustrating scenes from different periods of prehistoric life.

The twelve-mile Ruins Road includes two driving loops that pass a series of mesa-top pithouse and pueblo ruins and cliff house overlooks. Each stop on this drive has exhibits to explain points of interest. Self-guiding or guided tours can be taken of Cliff Palace, Balcony House, Spruce Tree House, and Square Tower House on Chapin Mesa; and Step House and Long House on Wetherill Mesa. The number of tours conducted each day varies with the seasonal schedule. A visit to Cliff Palace, the largest cliff dwelling in the Southwest, with over two hundred rooms and twenty-three kivas, is an archaeological high point. In summer, the Park Service holds campfire talks at Morfield campground and offers nature walks for children. Several hiking trails are also available.

Service concessions at Mesa Verde include motel (Far View Lodge), restaurant, cafeteria, gas station, general store, and laundromat. These concessions, it should be noted, are only open from mid-May to mid-October. The campground is usually open from June 1 to September 29. Travel facilities and overnight accommodations can also be found in Mancos, Cortez, and Durango. From any standpoint—archaeology, nature, scenery—Mesa Verde National Park is a wonderful place to see. It does, however, become noticeably crowded during peak summer months and people with a flexible travel schedule may find an off-season trip here more to their liking.

Suggested reading: *Understanding the Anasazi of Mesa Verde and Hovenweep,* School of American Research, Santa Fe, 1985.

Ute Mountain Ute Tribal Park

Ute Mountain Ute Tribal Park is located in Mancos Canyon near Towaoc, Colorado. Weekday tours of these back country Pueblo ruins are conducted by the Ute Mountain Tribe from mid-May through late October. To join a tour, drive south from Cortez eleven miles on U.S. 666 to the Ute Mountain Pottery Factory. Tours leave from here at 9:00 A.M. and return about 4:00 P.M.

When European-American settlers first established themselves in what is now southwestern Colorado, this region was the traditional territory of the Ute Indians. The Ute Mountain Ute Reservation now covers about 550,000 acres in an east-west strip south of Mesa Verde and north of the

New Mexico and Arizona borders. From around the time of Christ to circa 1300, this was Anasazi country, and the Utes are presently the custodians of many archaeological sites from this early Pueblo culture.

The Mancos Canyon tour, guided by a Ute Indian, is an unusual and fascinating archaeological experience in the reservation's back country. These ruins represent the same period and culture as those of nearby Mesa Verde, and were excavated in the mid-1970s by archaeologists from the University of Colorado under the direction of David A. Bredernitz. Although they were subsequently stabilized by the Ute Tribe, they still have a relatively rustic and pristine appearance, especially when compared to the more thoroughly cleaned up or reconstructed sites in the National Park system.

Non-Utes may visit Ute Mountain Ute Tribal Park only by taking an authorized tour. Tour members drive up the canyon in their own vehicles, stopping at several rock art sites and unexcavated surface pueblos on the way. They then proceed on foot along a one-and-a-half-mile trail to four cliff dwellings. This hike involves climbing up and down several ladders. During the tour, the guide explains the prehistory of the area and recent archaeological activities.

Cortez, Colorado, eleven miles to the north, offers travel facilities and overnight accommodations. Other nearby archaeological monuments include Mesa Verde National Park (see p. 31), Hovenweep National Monument (p. 37), Lowry Pueblo Ruins (p. 39), and the Escalante and Dominguez Ruins (p. 41).

Left: Holly Group,
Hovenweep National Monument

Hovenweep National Monument

Hovenweep National Monument straddles the border of southwestern Colorado and southeastern Utah. Monument headquarters are located at Square Tower Group on the graded dirt road between Pleasant View, 25 miles to the northeast, and Hatch Trading Post, 16 miles west in Utah.

The name *Hovenweep* comes from a Ute word meaning "deserted valley"; it is well chosen, for these scrubby mesas, cut by long empty canyons, seem to hold little promise for human subsistence. And yet, even today, despite their barren appearance, they support a few range cattle and a small population of Navajo. In addition, they are the object of intensive energy exploration and development.

Hovenweep National Monument consists of six clusters of ruins, four in Colorado and two in Utah, situated at the heads of box canyons. Monument headquarters is located at the Square Tower Group from which trails can be followed to numerous sites in Square Tower Canyon. Other ruins groups — Holly, Horseshoe, Hackberry, Cajon, and Cutthroat Castle — can be reached by driving several miles on unpaved roads. The Hovenweep ruins are unlike any others in the Southwest both in architecture and setting, and are fascinating to visit if one has the time to venture off the beaten track.

The Hovenweep people were part of the larger Anasazi culture that developed along the San Juan River and its tributaries in the Four Corners Region. Closely related to the peoples of Mesa Verde fifty-five miles to the east, they began establishing small farming settlements on the mesas and in the valleys around A.D. 1100. At this time, one should remember, there had

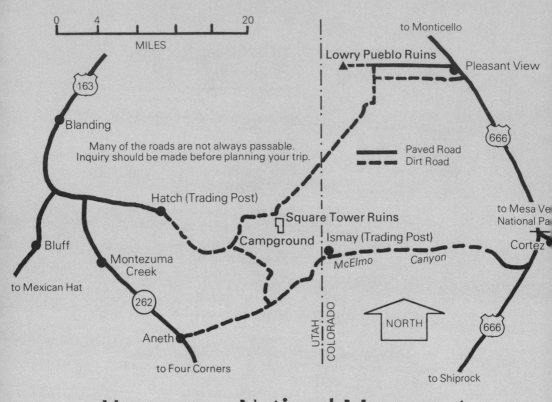

Hovenweep National Monument

been no overgrazing of the land and less soil erosion, and the pattern of rainfall may have been more advantageous for dry farming than it is today.

After A.D. 1200, the scattered Hovenweep settlements drew together to form larger pueblos at the heads of small draws and box canyons. Here, moisture that had percolated through the porous sandstone of the mesas to an impervious layer of shale flowed laterally underground to emerge at the canyon heads in the forms of springs and seeps. The Hovenweep settlers built check dams to control surface run-off and cultivated garden plots of corn, beans, and squash on the terraced slopes of the lower canyons. They also continued a long tradition of hunting and gathering.

Perhaps the most remarkable accomplishment of the Hovenweep people, at least to observers today, is their buildings. Around the rims of the canyons they constructed massive masonry pueblos, understandably referred to as "castles" by early explorers. And in the canyons, often just below the spring, they built tall stone towers whose principal purpose, it has been suggested, was to perplex archaeologists of a future age.

The square, oval, circular, and D-shaped towers of Hovenweep display expert masonry and engineering. Foundation leveling was a practice often ignored by these architects, some of whose structures are perched on great uneven chunks of fallen rimrock. Except for narrow peepholes, the towers are virtually

38

windowless and at least one has no door, apparently having been entered through the roof. Standing like timeless sentinels or guardians of some long forgotten treasure, their function has been the subject of much speculation. Did they guard the springs? Were they lookouts? Signal towers? Celestial observatories? Granaries? Water reservoirs? Habitations? Ceremonial innovations? All have been suggested; hopefully, some insightful future archaeologist will resolve the mystery of the Hovenweep towers.

Ruins in the Hovenweep area were first reported in 1854 by a Mormon expedition into southern Utah. Sixty-five years later, Jesse Walter Fewkes of the Smithsonian Institution published *Prehistoric Villages, Castles, and Towers of Southwestern Colorado,* an archaeological survey report describing many sites, including those within the monument. Since Fewkes's survey, surprisingly little archaeological work and no major excavations have been conducted here. Considering the unique character of these structures, it seems curious that so few details are known about their history and purpose.

Between 1276 and 1299, the northern Southwest was struck by a severe drought and the Hovenweep area was abandoned. It is thought that the people moved south and east to the Little Colorado River drainage and the Rio Grande in search of a more productive existence. The architectural monuments they left behind, even after seven centuries of weathering and many years of vandalism, testify to the extraordinary building skills of the Hovenweep Anasazi and exemplify the creative response of these people to an obviously challenging environment.

Hovenweep is a geographically disconnected monument. The small visitor center and ranger station are located at Square Tower Group, the largest and best preserved complex of ruins. Here one can pick up printed

directions to the outlying groups and information on particular sites. Also available is a detailed trail guide to Square Tower Group, including Hovenweep Castle, Hovenweep House, Square Tower, Talus Pueblo, and other archaeological and environmental features in the canyon. Persons interested in going to the outlying groups of ruins should check road conditions in wet weather. While visiting the sites, great care should be exercised not to disturb unstable walls or fragile masonry.

All approaches to Hovenweep National Monument are on unpaved roads that become slick in wet weather. There are no motels, restaurants, gas stations, or other services in this region. Inconvenience aside, Hovenweep is one of the most impressive archaeological preserves in the Southwest and offers a view of Anasazi life found nowhere else. For people staying at Mesa Verde, Cortez, Bluff, or Blanding, a trip here makes a good one-day excursion. Persons wishing to stay longer can use the monument's campground, which has fresh water and modern toilet facilities. Food and firewood must be brought in as neither is available at Hovenweep.

Lowry Pueblo Ruins

Lowry Pueblo Ruins are located in southwestern Colorado near the town of Pleasant View on U.S. 666. At Pleasant View, turn west and proceed 9 miles, following road signs to the site.

The county road from Pleasant View to Lowry Pueblo Ruins meanders through rolling hills and vales with pinto bean fields stretching in all directions. The land is fertile, well-watered,

Lowry Pueblo ruins

and productive, atypical of a south-western landscape.

Lowry Pueblo was built after A.D. 1090 by Anasazi people of Chacoan extraction and it represents what is probably the furthest Chacoan outlier to the north. As the pueblo's population increased over about twenty years to an estimated one hundred people, the pueblo was in a continual state of construction and remodeling. Its occupants, like their neighbors at Escalante, Mesa Verde, and Hovenweep, were farmers who supplemented a diet of corn, beans, and squash with the proceeds from hunting and gathering forays in the surrounding area. The pueblo reached a maximum size of forty rooms and included nine kivas and one great kiva situated a short distance away. Occupation here lasted only until about 1140, barely half a century, but no scientific evidence has emerged from the diggings to indicate a reason for abandonment. With no sign of warfare, internal strife, or natural disaster, archaeologists theorize that social and environmental factors were probably behind the inhabitants' decision to leave.

What remains of the pueblo today are one-story walls of admirable construction, with stones neatly cut and solidly laid in the Chacoan masonry tradition. The great kiva, which has been excavated and lies unroofed a short distance east of the pueblo, is a clue to Lowry's former importance as a religious center. To many people, however, the most interesting feature at this site is the painted kiva that is situated in one of the roomblocks. It was built around 1103 and its walls were decorated with painted designs on plaster. It has since been excavated, and is fitted with a modern roof to make a public exhibit. Unfortunately, the fragile murals are in a constant state of deterioration with a growing pile of painted plaster chips accumulating on the floor. Today one enters

the kiva through a side entrance, but its original users came down a ladder through a hatch in the roof.

Lowry Pueblo Ruins were not recorded until 1919, and even today the site is little known outside of archaeological circles. Apparently this site was missed by the 1776 Dominguez-Escalante Great Basin Expedition that camped nearby, missed again by the Hayden Expedition of 1881, and subsequently given little notice by local settlers. The site was named for George Lowry, an early homesteader, and was first excavated in the 1930s by Paul S. Martin of the Chicago Field Museum of Natural History. Today it is administered by the Bureau of Land Management.

As one approaches this site, one will notice the mounds of an unexcavated pueblo just off the road on the left. Lowry is a short distance further on. Facilities here include a small parking circle, picnic tables, a display case with site plan and printed brochures, and a trail through the ruins. The ruins are open daily.

Escalante and Dominguez Ruins

The Escalante and Dominguez Ruins are located in southwestern Colorado between Cortez and Dolores. From Cortez, take State Highway 145 north 8 miles and turn west on a county road leading to State 147. The monument is about 1 mile on the right.

On the 13th we made camp, both to allow the Padre to improve (Dominguez had a fever), and to take a bearing on the polar elevation of this site and meadow of El Rio de los Dolores where we found ourselves. ... Upon an elevation of the river's south side, there was in ancient times a small settlement of the same type as those of the Indians of New Mexico....

Fray Silvestre Velez de Escalante
1776

Sixteen days prior to making this notation in his journal, Silvestre de Escalante and Fray Francisco Atanacio Dominguez had set off from Santa Fe with eight men to find a new route to Monterey on the California coast. Their overnight stop on a hill overlooking the Dolores River gave them time to investigate the ruins of a small Anasazi pueblo, later to be named after Escalante, and to make the first record of an archaeological site in what is now the state of Colorado. Not mentioned by Escalante was an even smaller satellite pueblo near the southern base of the hill that would later commemorate his clerical partner, Fray Dominguez.

The Escalante Ruin is a twenty-five-room masonry pueblo situated at the southern end of this long hill. Below, the Dolores River turns sharply north creating a wide flood plain, and to the south, the low ridgeline of the Mesa Verde sits darkly on the horizon. This hilltop commands a wide view over the surrounding countryside contained by highlands to the east, south, and west, but extending far northward as plains and low rolling hills.

The Escalante Ruin was constructed and inhabited in the late eleventh century and continued to be occupied, with two periods of abandonment, until the beginning of the thirteenth century. Then, as today, the environment offered a variety of food resources, materials for building, tool manufacture, pottery, and plenty of water. Additionally, the site was situated along a trade route. Mule deer, antelope, elk, and bighorn sheep were plentiful and provided an important source of meat for these early inhabitants.

The architecture and layout of the Escalante Ruin is of Chacoan style.

The pueblo is rectangular in shape, eighty-two feet long by sixty-three feet wide, with a single kiva at center. Double rows of rooms are located on the east, north, and west sides, with a single row to the south. If the building style at Escalante is predominantly Chacoan, other cultural remains, notably pottery, reflect a strong influence from Mesa Verde. Anthropologists consider house construction to have been a principally male function in Pueblo society; ceramics, on the other hand, was a female activity. Consequently, it has been theorized that a group consisting principally of men from an area associated with Chaco Canyon came to this site in the late eleventh century, constructed the pueblo, and intermarried with women from nearby Mesa Verde. It seems clear from the archaeological record that over the generations, the Mesa Verde strain came to dominate the cultural expression of the community.

The Dominguez Ruin is one of a number of small sites around the southern base of the hill that was associated with Escalante Pueblo. Consisting of only four rooms and a kiva, it was evidently occupied by an extended family of eight or ten people beginning around A.D. 1123. This small site, probably of little note in its time and certainly unimpressive to look at today, contained one of the most interesting human burials ever found in the Southwest—the burial of a man thought by archaeologists to have been of considerably high status as indicated by a collection of jewelry and other artifacts interred with him. Few such burials have ever been found in the Southwest—one of the reasons why prehistoric Pueblo people are believed to have had an egalitarian society—but it is highly doubtful that we will ever know who this individual was.

The excavations of the Escalante and Dominguez Ruins were carried out as an American Bicentennial project and coincided with the two hundredth anniversary of their discovery.

Escalante ruins

Stabilization and interpretation of the sites were ongoing at the time of this writing and are expected to be completed in the early 1980s. Present facilities consist of a parking lot, toilet, picnic table, small historical exhibit, and a paved pathway leading up the hill to the Escalante Ruin. The walk up the hill takes about ten minutes and is worthwhile not only for the archaeological experience but also for the lovely view attained from the top. The Dominguez Ruin lies adjacent to the parking lot.

The town of Cortez has numerous travel services including motels and restaurants. Mesa Verde National Park (see p. 31), Hovenweep National Monument (p. 37), and the Lowry Pueblo Ruins (p. 39) are all within a relatively short drive.

Suggested reading: *The Archaeology and Stabilization of the Dominguez and Escalante Ruins.* Colorado State Office, Bureau of Land Management, 1979.

Three Kiva Pueblo

Three Kiva Pueblo is located on the Montezuma Canyon road in southeastern Utah approximately 15 miles north of Hatch Trading Post and 23 miles south of the intersection with U.S. 163 south of Monticello. From Blanding, a gravel road leads east to Montezuma Canyon at a point about 6 miles south of the site. More detailed information can be obtained from the offices of the Bureau of Land Management in Monticello.

Three Kiva Pueblo, a fourteen-room Anasazi habitation located in Montezuma Canyon about twenty-two miles south of the Abajo Mountains in southeastern Utah, is an out-of-the-way Indian ruin that will probably be more rewarding for people with a special interest in archaeology and exploring to visit than for casual tourists.

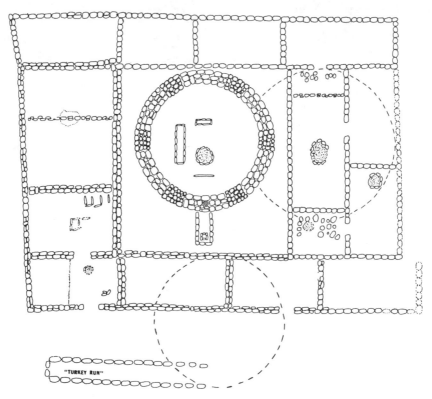

Three Kiva Pueblo ground plan, prepared by Donald E. Miller

This is an arid and unpopulated stretch of country whose scenic charm lies in contrasts between the spare rugged mesas and the arroyos shaded by willows and cottonwoods. Much of this land belongs to Ute and Navajo Indians, the successors to the Anasazi whose presence here dates back more than a millenium.

Three Kiva is reached by an unimproved dirt road that crisscrosses Montezuma Creek at numerous points just south of the site. At these intersections one must traverse wide expanses of deep sand deposited by past flooding, an experience not recommended to anyone without a four-wheel drive vehicle. The author himself spent the better part of a day

at one of these lonely spots, digging out his car by hand and wondering, as his perspiration evaporated in the desert heat, how he ever became interested in southwestern prehistory.

The first archaeological reconnaissance of Montezuma Canyon was made in 1886 by the noted American photographer and explorer William H. Jackson. Excavations on nearby Alcali Ridge were carried out in 1908 and again in the 1930s. Three Kiva Pueblo was excavated between 1969 and 1972 by the Brigham Young University Field School of Archaeology.

The first section of Three Kiva Pueblo was built in the ninth century A.D. The site experienced three occupations and building phases and was abandoned around A.D. 1300. Its earliest occupants appear to have been culturally associated with the Kayenta branch of the Anasazi, whose central territory lay some distance to the south. But later, the Three Kiva people were more closely related to those at Mesa Verde and nearby Hovenweep. The rooms of this pueblo form a neat square. Windblown fill on the kiva floor under the collapsed roof measured over two feet in depth, indicating that the kiva survived intact for a long period after the pueblo's abandonment. Just to the south of the pueblo is an interesting two-by-twenty-foot masonry room believed to have been a "turkey run." The abundance of turkey bones in this area was a good clue as to its function and indicated the significant role this domestic bird played as a source of meat and feathers.

During excavations of this site, two abalone shell pendants were found, evidence of trade contact with the Pacific Coast. Many stone artifacts were also found, including knives, scrapers, drills, projectile points, hammerstones, hoes, axes, mauls, dishes, manos, and metates. From objects such as these, archaeologists are able to reconstruct a picture of the activities of the pueblo's inhabitants.

Although travel to Three Kiva Pueblo can present a problem, the site has been prepared for visitation by the Bureau of Land Management and a trip here would be worthwhile for anyone strongly interested in the archaeology of this area. Bring water, food, and a shovel, just in case.

Suggested reading: "A Synthesis of Excavations at Site 42SA863, Three Kiva Pueblo, Montezuma Canyon, San Juan County, Utah," by Donald E. Miller, 1974. Masters thesis available through Brigham Young University.

Newspaper Rock

Newspaper Rock, a State Historic Monument in southeastern Utah, is located on the north side of Route 211, about 12 miles west of the intersection with U.S. 163 north of Monticello.

Panels of rock art are always particularly impressive, and Newspaper Rock is one of the finest examples to be found. Here, etched into the dark patina of a single smooth rock slab, are literally hundreds of figures protected from the elements by a natural overhang that seems to have been custom-made for the purpose. These pictures were produced over a period of more than three thousand years by Archaic, Basketmaker, and Fremont people, by Pueblo, Ute, and Navajo Indians, and by Hispanic and Anglo settlers.

Dating presents a major though not totally insurmountable challenge to students of Indian rock art. The most accurate way of determining a time frame for this artistic expression is when petroglyphs or rock paintings are clearly associated with other cultural material of a known date. Petroglyphs and paintings, for example, sometimes occur in or close to a cliff dwelling or other habitation site. This was not the case at Newspaper Rock where other dating methods must be employed. Observers will note the presence of horses and riders and realize that since the horse was introduced to North America by the Spanish, these particular images must date later than 1540. Historians would probably date the presence of horses in southeastern Utah after the late 1600s.

Scholars have given rough timeframes to certain styles of rock art. Some of the Newspaper Rock images are believed to go back at least to

Newspaper Rock detail

2000 B.C. Others can be related by style and subject matter to particular cultural groups whose presence in this area has been researched at other archaeological sites. Rock art scholars are slowly building up a body of knowledge about this phenomenon that traditionally has been given little serious consideration by archaeologists. But while the science of rock art research builds momentum and respectability, the pictures from antiquity remain on the rocks for ordinary people to see and appreciate for themselves. The images have a life and meaning of their own. Some are clear, some inscrutable; some have great artistic merit, others seem carelessly scrawled; some tell a story, others make a brief statement about an event, an animal, or person. Newspaper Rock can be seen in a minute or in an hour.

Suggested reading: *Indian Rock Art of the Southwest,* by Polly Schaafsma. School of American Research, Santa Fe, and University of New Mexico Press, Albuquerque, New Mexico, 1980.

Fremont rock art panel, the Maze, Canyonlands National Park. Courtesy of the School of American Research. Photograph by Karl Kernberger.

Canyonlands National Park

The Needles District of Canyonlands National Park is located at the end of State 211, northwest of Monticello, Utah.

Like the Grand Canyon, Canyonlands is an area (525 square miles) of extraordinary scenic and geologic beauty. The land here has been carved and shaped by forces of erosion for millions of years. But Canyonlands was once the home of prehistoric American Indians who left their mark here in the form of small scattered pueblo sites and cliff dwellings and also in some of the most striking examples of rock art to be found anywhere in North America. Although Canyonlands was not established as a national park with particular thought to the area's cultural heritage, many visitors will find it rewarding to explore the park's jeep and hiking trails with an archaeological orientation. The present guide will offer a general picture of the area's prehistory, little as it is

47

known, and suggest some places to visit, but persons interested in archaeological sites should first talk with park rangers, consult local trail maps, and allow plenty of time for personal explorations.

Certain areas of the southern portion of the park, known as the Needles District, were inhabited by Pueblo people who migrated north from the Four Corners region beginning about A.D. 950. Their economy was based on farming and therefore their settlements were established in areas with arable land and dependable sources of water. These Anasazi also hunted game and had a thorough knowledge of wild edible plants and seeds. The places they found suitable for habitation were small and scattered, and their population, estimated to have reached a peak of about one thousand people, was never concentrated into large communities. The Anasazi resided in the Canyonlands area for about three hundred years. Droughts of the thirteenth century, which plagued the entire Southwest, finally caused them to abandon their homes here and move to areas with more dependable water. Their sites were never reoccupied.

The most accessible archaeological site in the park is Roadside Ruin, located one-eighth of a mile off the paved road about one mile west of the Needles District ranger station. Roadside Ruin (not really a ruin since it is in nearly perfect condition) is a masonry storage bin built in the shelter of an overhanging rock. It is easy to view, and although unimpressive in size, is remarkable for its pristine condition. The site is well marked along the road.

Particularly rich archaeologically are Salt Canyon, Horse Canyon, Ruins Park, and the Maze, all of which can be visited by jeep or on foot. Here there are cliff houses and small granaries tucked in rock shelters, petroglyphs, and galleries with dozens of elaborate and colorful rock paintings. These paintings are dominated by tall anthropomorphic figures whose appearance often resembles ghosts or mummies. Figures of varying size and intensity provide a sense of three dimensionality as if they were receding into or emerging from the rock itself. Who painted these awesome creatures? Some archaeologists classify them as Fremont — the region was generally occupied by Fremont people between approximately A.D. 700 to 1200 — but Polly Schaafsma, who has studied this rock art in depth and defined its style, ascribes it to pre-Fremont hunting and gathering peoples. As artists, they used a variety of painterly techniques to gain special effects, from spattering paint, applying paint directly with their fingers, using yucca brushes, to blowing pigment through reed tubes and incising lines through painted areas to achieve texture. Most pigment is dark reddish, often faded, but some figures are decorated with white lines. The rock paintings at Canyonlands express a heightened sense of spirituality and mysticism, qualities inherent in much rock art in the Southwest and, for that matter, in art generally throughout the world. The artwork of these deep canyons represents a very precious American cultural treasure; hopefully it will be treated with care and respect for future generations to appreciate.

The Needles District of Canyonlands has a visitor center, staff of rangers, and campground. People planning to drive the jeep trails will need four-wheel drive vehicles and provisions suitable for going into rugged back country. Water, especially in certain seasons, is scarce in the canyons. The nearest towns with travel services and overnight accommodations are Moab and Monticello.

Right: Roadside ruin, Canyonlands National Park

Edge of the Cedars ruins

Edge of the Cedars State Historical Monument

Edge of the Cedars State Historical Monument is located in the southeastern Utah town of Blanding, between Bluff and Monticello, on U.S. 163. Street directions to the monument are clearly marked in Blanding.

One of the most recently established archaeological monuments in the Southwest is a combination anthropological-historical museum and archaeological site in Blanding, Utah. Excavations at the Edge of the Cedars site were begun in the late 1960s and, in 1978, the ruins and associated museum were opened to the public. As of the present writing, only a small portion of the site has been excavated and findings have not as yet been published.

50

The pueblo ruins are located near the northern periphery of the Anasazi cultural area and were occupied between roughly A.D. 750 and 1220. They are situated on a ridge overlooking Westwater Canyon, which is still a reliable source of water, and south of the Abajo Mountains, an important hunting and gathering area.

Edge of the Cedars consists of six complexes or blocks of rooms, a dozen kivas, and one great kiva. Great kivas probably served a broader function than regular kivas, and were used by the entire community rather than by a more limited group or clan. The great kiva at this site is unexcavated and appears as a large shallow depression in the ground. Another kiva, however, has been excavated and reconstructed and may be entered by means of a rooftop ladder.

In 1969, a copper bell was excavated at this site, tangible evidence of trading links with Indian groups in Mexico far to the south, the only area where such an object could have been manufactured in prehistoric times.

Edge of the Cedars museum, open daily from 9:00 A.M. to 5:00 P.M., contains exhibits relating to the various cultures that have affected this region of southeastern Utah. These include the Anasazi, who built and occupied the pueblo, the Navajo and Ute Indians, and early Anglo settlers. A trail leads through the site and can be followed with the help of a printed trail guide explaining archaeological features along the way. The ruins walk takes about ten or fifteen minutes. This site has great potential as an archaeological exhibit and, as it is further developed and interpreted, may prove to be one of the most fascinating monuments in the area.

Blanding is a small Mormon town with several cafes, gas stations, and other travel facilities. Other nearby archaeological sites are Newspaper Rock (see p. 45), Westwater Ruin (p. 51), Three Kiva Pueblo (p. 43), and Mule Canyon Ruins (p. 53).

Westwater Ruin

To find Westwater Ruin, take U.S. 163 south out of Blanding for 1.25 miles, then turn right on a paved road. The sign at this intersection reads "Scenic View—2." The Westwater Ruin overlook is 2 miles from the turnoff.

Just south of Blanding, Utah, an Anasazi cliff dwelling sits tucked in a large picturesque rock alcove along the west wall of Westwater Canyon. Lush undergrowth on the canyon floor engulfs a small, flowing creek, suggesting the desirability of this spot to the prehistoric occupants of the pueblo. The canyon has other ruins, including the much larger Edge of the Cedars Pueblo upstream.

A tree ring core taken in 1936 from a Westwater roof beam revealed a date of 1243, but the site is believed to have been occupied as early as A.D. 750 and abandoned around 1300. Its occupants were generally related to the Mesa Verde Anasazi to the southeast. The site consists of thirteen ground-level rooms plus an undetermined number of second story rooms and five kivas. These habitations were divided into two main roomblocks under the cliff.

Westwater is one of uncounted archaeological sites in the Southwest that have been heavily damaged by pothunters, vandals, and careless visitors. Walls have been pushed over and undermined, building stones scattered, and holes dug in the floor fill. What remains are a few knee- and waist-high pueblo walls.

A short steep path leads from the overlook parking lot to the ruin. The poor condition of this cliff dwelling, however, and the absence of interpretation will disappoint many people who choose to make the walk across the canyon.

Mule Canyon
Indian Ruins

Mule Canyon Indian Ruins are located about 16 miles east of Natural Bridges National Monument and 28 miles west of Blanding, Utah. The site is a well-marked rest stop along the north side of Interstate 95.

Mule Canyon Indian Ruins are located in southeastern Utah about twenty-five miles north of the San Juan River. The pueblo here was inhabited in the eleventh and twelfth centuries during a time when Anasazi culture was at its height and was penetrating far into southern Utah.

Mule Canyon Pueblo consisted of twelve masonry rooms, two kivas, and a tower, and is believed to have been the home of one or two extended families including perhaps eight adults plus their children. The roomblock was used for living, for storage of food and supplies, and as a work area in bad weather. Most daily activities, however, took place on the rooftops and in the plaza in front of the pueblo. A tunnel or crawlway led from the residential area to a masonry kiva that today is the site's most impressive structure. Entrance to the kiva was also made by means of a roof hatch. Kiva features include a wall niche, foot drum, pilasters to support roof beams, firepit, stone deflector, and ventilator shaft. A second tunnel is believed to have fulfilled a defensive function and to have been used for visual communications with other towers in the vicinity.

Travelers on I-95 will find a tour of these prehistoric ruins to be an interesting fifteen-minute stopover. Here one can visualize to some extent how, in this scenic but presently unin-

Left: Kiva, Mule Canyon Indian Ruins

habited region, a Pueblo family lived eight centuries ago. Although little archaeological interpretation is offered at the site, the structures themselves suggest a story that anyone can appreciate. The discovery and excavation of this site were a by-product of the construction of the I-95 highway that runs northwest from near Blanding, across the Colorado River to Hanksville. The nearest travel services are to be found in Blanding or Bluff.

Natural Bridges
National Monument

Natural Bridges National Monument is located along Interstate 95, 26 miles east of Fry Canyon and 42 miles west of Blanding, in southeastern Utah.

In 1908, President Theodore Roosevelt set aside over seven thousand acres of land around upper White Canyon, Utah, as a national monument to safeguard three natural sandstone bridges of unusual beauty. Included in this protected area, however, were a large number of prehistoric archaeological sites. White Canyon, in addition to having a series of extraordinary geologic formations, also was a haven of the Anasazi Indians for over one thousand years.

The Natural Bridges site was first recorded at the late date of 1883. This is a rugged and relatively inhospitable region of the Southwest that until recent times was penetrated by only a few explorers, surveyors, and pioneers, and left largely unsettled. Archaeological research was carried out only on a small scale until 1961, when a major survey of the upper White Canyon area was completed. This survey reported 200 archaeological sites and identified an Anasazi occupation of the area from the first

Handprints, Kachina Bridge, Natural Bridges National Monument

centuries A.D. to about 1300. These sites included many collapsed and buried structures on the juniper- and sage-covered mesas, as well as pueblos, kivas, granaries, petroglyphs, and rock paintings in the inner canyon. Some of the cliff-sheltered pueblos have survived in excellent condition, even with roofs intact, a clue that they had been abandoned abruptly, without violence, and with no later reoccupation, remodeling, or recycling of building materials. Also contributing to their fine preservation was the fact that in the historic period, this locality had never been the home of Navajos, Utes, or Anglos. In fact, it has been left virtually undisturbed for at least six centuries.

Regular use of White Canyon may have begun as early as two thousand years ago. Certainly from around A.D. 450, the canyon witnessed a stable population with a particular influx of people and a building spurt in the mid-1100s. Artifacts found during surveys and excavations suggest that the area's inhabitants enjoyed close cultural ties with Mesa Verde communities and probably carried on fairly active trading with Anasazi peoples from the Kayenta district to the south. One interesting phenomenon that archaeologists have noted in the course of their research here and elsewhere on the northern periphery of the Anasazi country is a culture lag

relative to contemporaneous sites in the middle San Juan River region, the Anasazi heartland. This lag is comparable to what occurs in present-day American society when, for example, a fashionable trend in New York City or San Francisco takes a period of time to catch hold elsewhere.

The last tree-ring date at Natural Bridges is 1251 — the last year when, as near as can be determined, a tree was felled for use in house building. Diminished construction presumably reflected a decline in population. During the same period, the Anasazi world generally was undergoing change and disruption. Like so many sites, the settlements at Natural Bridges were victims of the calamitous events that exacted a heavy toll in the Four Corners region and beyond during the thirteenth century.

Natural Bridges was set aside as a geologic preserve, and an eight-mile paved driving loop leads to scenic overlooks at Sipapu, Kachina, and Owachomo Bridges. Archaeological sites are not interpreted but can be reached by hiking the switchback trails in and out of White Canyon. The main trail begins along the roadside at Sipapu Bridge and follows the canyon to Kachina Bridge. A short distance down this trail, on the right hand side just downstream from Deer Canyon, Horsecollar Ruins are visible. At Kachina Bridge, a number of ancient mud huts can be seen in the shelter of a broad rock overhang, on which several good examples of rock art are visible. One of these is a well-preserved row of painted handprints, a popular Anasazi motif and a clear statement of the identity and presence of their makers. At Grand Gulch, a primitive area south of Natural Bridges, a long wall covered with handprints is known as "the FBI panel." Most of the rock art in White Canyon dates from the Pueblo period—A.D. 950 to 1300. There are other archaeological sites in the canyon that, with a little time and effort, can be sought out by interested persons. Rangers at the monument can give specific directions to these areas and will no doubt caution visitors about the fragility of these ruins and the need to preserve them for the future.

The monument has a visitor center with interpretive exhibits and a slide program on the area's geology. A campground is available, but no food, gas, or camping supplies. The nearest points to obtain these are at Fry Canyon, Blanding, and Mexican Hat. Grand Gulch (see p. 67) is located only a few miles south on Highway 261, and Mule Canyon Ruins (p. 53) are about sixteen miles east on the way to Blanding.

Suggested reading: *An Archaeological Survey of the Upper White Canyon Area, Southeastern Utah,* by Philip M. and Audrey E. Hobler. Utah State Historical Society, 1978.

Anasazi Indian Village State Historical Monument

Anasazi Indian Village State Historical Monument is located about 2 miles north of the small village of Boulder in south central Utah. Follow Utah 12 from Bryce Canyon National Park 75 miles east through Tropic and Escalante to Boulder. From Capitol Reef National Park on Utah 24, take the unpaved but scenic road near Torrey south 38 miles to Boulder.

When Kayenta Anasazi people established a village around A.D. 1075 off the southern edge of the Aquarius Plateau in what is now southern Utah, they had every reason to anticipate a prosperous existence. The area had fertile soils, reliable streams, plentiful game, abundant firewood, and materials for house building and the manufacturing of pottery, tools, utensils, and clothing. Even the climate was good—pleasant in summer, not too harsh in winter. Compared to settlements in the Grand Canyon to the south, life at this Kayenta outpost was relatively easy.

Once established, the occupants of this village carried on farming along the streams and in irrigated fields, hunted game ranging from bighorn sheep and mule deer to rabbits, and gathered many wild edible plants and seeds. Although they brought with them customs and traits from their Kayenta region of origin, they soon were influenced by local Fremont people and by other Anasazi groups. Archaeologists believe the village, known in archaeological literature as the Coombs site, functioned as a cultural crossroads between Kayenta populations to the south and neighboring groups of central and western Utah.

The Coombs village thrived until about A.D. 1275 when it was almost completely consumed by fire. What caused the conflagration is impossible to determine today; it could have been accidental, intentional, or perhaps the result of warfare. Another mystery is where the Coombs people went after the disaster. As yet, no sites have been excavated that show a later occupation by these people. Perhaps they broke up into small groups and

Coombs Village circa A.D. 1100, Anasazi Indian Village State Historical Monument. Restoration by George A. King.

Restored building of Coombs Village. Photograph by Matts Myhrman.

returned south and east to join other Anasazi peoples in the San Juan River drainage. Their village, soon to be covered by dust and blowing sand, lay undisturbed for seven centuries.

The Coombs site was excavated in the 1950s as part of a large archaeological salvage project resulting from the planned, now completed, Glen Canyon Dam. Although the waters of Lake Powell lie forty-five miles distant, excavation of this site, the largest Anasazi ruins west of the Colorado River, was deemed essential in trying to better understand the prehistory of the inundated region which itself had few sites.

The Coombs site is administered as part of Anasazi Indian Village State Historical Monument, which includes a visitor center, museum, and picnic area. The monument is open daily on a year-round basis. The nearest travel services are to be found in Escalante, the next town south on Route 12.

Navajo National Monument

Navajo National Monument is located in northeastern Arizona. To reach this monument, follow U.S. 160 northeastward 50 miles from Tuba City or southwestward 22 miles from Kayenta. At this point, a 9-mile paved road leads to the monument.

Keet Seel, in Tsegi Canyon, is the largest cliff dwelling in Arizona and one of the best preserved. Betatakin, in a Tsegi side canyon, is only slightly smaller—135 rooms—but viewed from a distant overlook at Navajo National Monument it appears miniature and fragile in relation to the high-vaulted rock alcove that shelters it. These are two of the most beautiful prehistoric ruins in the Southwest. Far from major highways, in a remote canyon-cut sector of the Navajo reservation, they require a significant commitment of time and energy to fully appreciate.

The inhabitants of Keet Seel and Betatakin were Kayenta Anasazi. The Kayenta district, along with Mesa Verde and Chaco Canyon, comprised one of the three core areas where prehistoric Pueblo culture flourished. Like other Anasazi, the Kayenta people emerged out of an older Basketmaker tradition to become successful farmers, builders, and craftsmen. In the eleventh, twelfth, and early thirteenth centuries, the Kayenta cultural territory spread out over the western flank of the San Juan region, reaching west as far as the Grand Canyon and north into southern Utah. But in the mid-to late 1200s, their pattern of existence was upset by environmental and social events, resulting in profound adjustments— the relocation of many communities and building of cliff dwellings, and ultimately the abandonment of the entire San Juan region. This frenzied period in Anasazi pre-history has fascinated generations of archaeologists and is likely to remain a subject of study for years to come. The inhabitants of Keet Seel and Betatakin were caught in the middle of this disturbing period.

Betatakin and Keet Seel were built and occupied in the 1260s and 1270s, occupied for thirty to forty years, and abandoned around A.D. 1300. One may reasonably wonder why people would relocate here and expend such energy and creativity only to move on a generation or two later. One respected theory is that formerly productive farming areas in the alluvial valleys further down the canyon were rendered useless in the mid-thirteenth century by a change from winter-dominant precipitation, characterized by gentle rains and snows, to a pattern of heavy summer thunderstorms. Ensuing sheet erosion caused widespread arroyo-cutting, lowering of water tables, and decreasing agricultural productivity. These problems

Betatakin ruins, Navajo National Monument

were then compounded later in the century by drought. In response, the small scattered communities of the Kayenta district consolidated into larger villages close to reliable water sources near the heads of canyons. This new way of life, however, was successful only for a short time; consequently, the cliff dwellers— numbering about seven hundred in Tsegi Canyon—were obliged to search elsewhere for a more dependable subsistence. Many are thought to have migrated south to the area of the Hopi Mesas.

Betatakin, observable from an overlook near the headquarters of Navajo National Monument, is the more accessible of the two ruins, and guided tours (no reservations taken) are conducted to this site on a daily basis from approximately April through September. Usually, three tours, each including up to twenty people, are led every day. The round trip takes about three hours and includes a seven-hundred-foot return climb. The trail to Betatakin winds down to the canyon floor, leads through stands of scrub oak and lush vegetational growth, crosses a stream, and climbs up the talus slope to the site. The ruins are strung along a long ledge—in Navajo, Betatakin means "Ledge House"—in the protection of a five-hundred-foot cliff overhang. While at Betatakin, one can walk through the ruins viewing Anasazi houses along the way. The author happened to visit Betatakin once during a brief, late summer shower to find the pueblo perfectly sheltered with numerous thin waterfalls pouring over the cliff from the slickrock mesa above.

Betatakin is believed to have been planned and constructed as an entire unit, then occupied by a single group of people. When the ruins were discovered in 1907 by John Wetherill and Byron Cummings, they were in excellent condition and contained a large collection of artifacts.

Keet Seel was discovered by Richard Wetherill, the Mancos,

Colorado, rancher who also found Cliff Palace at Mesa Verde. The site has 155 rooms and six kivas and, like Betatakin, is tucked under the shelter of a large cliff alcove. The pueblo looks out over a lovely valley complete with stream, cottonwood groves, and meadows. Keet Seel is reached by means of a rough eight-mile trail up Tsegi and Keet Seel canyons.

Keet Seel's oldest section predates Betatakin by about seventeen years, but the pueblo's main building activity occurred in the 1270s. The excellent preservation of this site gives it the impression of having been abandoned much more recently than seven-hundred years ago. The roof beams of most rooms are intact, and archaeologists have obtained such precise tree-ring dates as to be able to reconstruct the building sequence of the site room by room.

The trip to Keet Seel can be made on foot or horseback. In order to allow enough time to see the ruins, relax, and enjoy the countryside, hikers should consider making this a two-day excursion with an overnight stay at the Keet Seel campground. Horseback riders can hire their mounts from Navajos through the monument headquarters and should plan to go and return the same day. Visitation to Keet Seel is limited to twenty persons per day in summer (fifteen hundred persons per summer), and both hikers and riders would be wise to make reservations for the trip in advance. The site is closed in winter; the schedule depends on weather and staff availability.

Navajo National Monument contains another well-known cliff dwelling— Inscription House. Unfortunately, the instability of this ruin has necessitated its being closed for an indefinite period. When reopened, this cliff dwelling can be reached by hiking approximately one and a half miles from a point near Inscription House Trading Post.

The monument has a visitor center with cultural exhibits and interpretive

Keet Seel ruins, Navajo National Monument

slide program, picnic areas, and a campground. Campfire talks on the archaeology, history, and natural history of the monument are held in summer. A schedule of tours to Betatakin is posted at the visitor center. People on a tight schedule may want to call ahead to find out departure times. Gas is available along U.S. 160; travel services and overnight accommodations can be found at Kayenta.

Suggested reading: *Tse Yaa Kin: House Beneath the Rock*, School of American Research, Santa Fe, 1986.

Petroglyph of Kokopelli, Sand Island Petroglyph Site

Sand Island Petroglyph Site

The Sand Island Petroglyph Site is located along the San Juan River about 2 miles west of Bluff, Utah, on U.S. 163. The turn-off from the highway to the site is well marked.

The San Juan River rises in the mountains of south-central Colorado, dips down into northwestern New Mexico, bends north to flow past the Four Corners into southeastern Utah, and continues west to Lake Powell where its waters mingle with those of the Colorado. As the principal drainage of the Colorado Plateau, the San Juan and its tributaries were a central factor in the development of Anasazi culture.

61

The more than twenty thousand archaeological sites that have been recorded in the San Juan Basin are the result of fifteen hundred years of Anasazi activity in the region.

The Sand Island petroglyph site looks out over the San Juan River several miles west of Bluff, Utah. This is the Anasazi heartland. Grand Gulch lies to the west, Mesa Verde to the east, Tsegi Canyon (Navajo National Monument) to the southwest, and Chaco Canyon to the southeast. Sand Island is one of the largest, most easily accessible rock art panels in the Southwest and includes scores of Basketmaker and Pueblo petroglyphs. Figures range from animals, birds, and masks, to geometric designs and abstract signs, doodles, and a fine example of Kokopelli, the hump-backed flute player, sporting an outrageously enlarged phallus. Kokopelli is a well-known character in prehistoric Indian art, always lively and virile, a constant symbol of fertility.

A cyclone fence has been constructed around the Sand Island panel to protect it from vandalism. This unfortunate necessity creates a barrier between viewer and art that will frustrate the near-sighted and disappoint the photographer. Close by is an attractive, rustic campground sheltered by cottonwoods, and the small Mormon community of Bluff is only two miles east on U.S. 163. Bluff has one or two gas stations, cafes, and a tourist lodge and is a good jumping-off place for trips to Mesa Verde (see p. 31), Hovenweep (p. 37), Natural Bridges (p. 53), and Navajo National Monument (p. 57), as well as other scenic and historic spots. Monument Valley and Valley of the Gods can be enjoyed from a car window; others, such as Grand Gulch (see p. 67), Poncho House, and the Goosenecks, can only be reached by foot, horseback, boat, or jeep. Quite apart from its archaeological resources, this general area boasts some of the most beautiful landscape in North America, and even the most harried travelers will find it hard not to linger.

Grand Canyon National Park

Grand Canyon National Park in northern Arizona can be approached from its south or north rims. The South Rim is located along State 64, 57 miles north of Interstate 40 at Williams. Another possible route is Highway 180 north of Flagstaff, which intersects with the state highway 28 miles from the entrance to the park. The north rim headquarters are at the end of State 67, 44 miles south of Jacob Lake. The North Rim is closed from about mid-October to about mid-May.

Grand Canyon is a window into time past. Its colorful rock strata, descending thousands of feet to the Colorado River, represent the hours of a regressive clock whose hands move slower than our minds can comprehend. Within its long hour of geologic time, Grand Canyon's human story accounts for only seconds.

Over recent decades, archaeologists have found a curious type of artifact buried in the recesses of a few canyon caves. Known as split-twig figurines, these objects are small effigies, probably of mountain sheep, carefully made of split and twisted twigs of willow or cottonwood sometimes in combination with grass or bark. Examples have been found symbolically speared by a miniature twig or with a pellet of dung pushed into their cavities. The figurines have been dated to around 2000 B.C. and are believed to be magic objects that played a part in the rituals of hunters who roamed the desert Southwest long before knowl-

Grand Canyon from South Rim, Grand Canyon National Park

edge of agriculture or the development of houses.

After the figurine era, the next evidence of man in the Grand Canyon dates to around A.D. 500, when a very small Basketmaker population was present. By A.D. 700, a few Pueblo farming settlements had been established on the South Rim, and within two centuries, the North Rim also was being settled. This population increased gradually for the next one hundred-fifty years.

In the mid-eleventh century, large numbers of Anasazi began moving to the Grand Canyon to establish small communities on its rims and plateaus and near arable deltas in the inner canyon. Their move was encouraged by a period of increased rainfall that made crop raising feasible in the hot arid climate along the Colorado River. Very likely, the new settlers alternated seasonally between a life on the rims and at the canyon bottom. With an altitude differential of up to 5,600 feet,

use of both areas for farming would have enabled them to greatly lengthen their overall annual growing season, thereby producing enough food to survive. While the Anasazi were living in the Grand Canyon, Cohonina people, whose culture was similar though less elaborate, also began inhabiting the region.

Archaeologists know of approximately two thousand sites in Grand Canyon. Of these, about fifteen hundred were inhabited between A.D. 1050 and 1150. This period, then — at least until recent years — represents the climax of the canyon's human story; afterwards, the Anasazi departed, moving back to the east, probably to the area of the Hopi Mesas. Oraibi, on Third Mesa, was founded around A.D. 1200, and until recent times the Hopi returned regularly to the canyon to collect salt and visit a mineral spring along the Little Colorado that they believe to be the Sipapu, or original place of emergence of human and animal life. Grand Canyon has been known to humans for about four millenia, but even during its peak period of occupation, it was a frontier where life was tenuous, and thriving settlements of one decade might sit as silent ghost towns the next.

There are three archaeological sites at Grand Canyon that have been excavated and opened to public visitation. Tusayan Ruin, located on the South Rim along the well-traveled road between Grand Canyon Village and Desert View, is probably the most heavily visited archaeological site in the Southwest. It is a small, unimposing ruin consisting of a few room walls and the remains of a kiva. Tusayan was built in the last decade or two of the twelfth century and did not survive long into the thirteenth century. This pueblo, which housed about thirty people, was active after the main period of Anasazi occupation of the Grand Canyon. Perhaps its inhabitants were among the last stragglers still eking out a living under trying conditions; if so, they only succeeded for about two generations, after which they, too, departed in search of better prospects.

Tusayan originally consisted of a U-shaped roomblock containing eight living units plus storage rooms and a kiva. When the kiva burned, another was built on the village trash mound a short distance south of the plaza. This is the kiva that can be viewed along the ruins trail today. The trash mound location apparently was chosen to give the kiva greater depth since bedrock lies only inches beneath the ground surface of the entire area. The kiva nevertheless was poorly constructed out of slanting wall timbers with upright posts supporting a brushwork and dirt roof. Both Tusayan kivas were excavated in the 1930s by Emil Haury, a noted southwestern archaeologist who later became widely known for his work at

Snaketown, a Hohokam village in southern Arizona.

Tusayan Ruin, located three miles west of Desert View, can be seen at any time by following a short self-guiding trail that begins at the parking lot along the road. Tusayan Museum has interpretive exhibits of the site as it may have appeared around A.D. 1185. The museum is open from 7:00 A.M. to 6:00 P.M. in summer, and from 8:00 A.M. to 5:00 P.M. in winter and early spring. Regular archaeological talks on Grand Canyon's prehistory are given at 10:30 A.M., 1:30 P.M., and 3:30 P.M. during summer hours and at 10:30 A.M. and 3:30 P.M. the rest of the year.

During the summers of 1969 and 1970, Douglas W. Schwartz of the School of American Research led an archaeological expedition to investigate the Walhalla Plateau on the North Rim. Of the eighty-four sites found, twenty-three were tested or excavated and one, Walhalla Glades Ruin, was stabilized and added to the park's interpretive program. The site consists of the remains of four masonry rooms and was probably the home of an extended Anasazi family after the mid-1000s. It is located across the road from Walhalla Glades Overlook, twenty-four miles from Grand Canyon Lodge and two miles from Cape Royal. The North Rim is closed during the winter, but in summer, the Park Service conducts a program called the Cliff Springs Walk, which goes by the Walhalla Glades Ruin and another small surface site and offers an interpretation of the area's prehistory.

Although some Basketmaker artifacts have been found on the Walhalla Plateau, the area is not thought to have experienced much human occupation until the tenth century, when Anasazi settlers built scattered agricultural field houses for grain

Right: Tusayan ruins, Grand Canyon National Park

Reconstruction of Bright Angel Pueblo, Grand Canyon National Park

storage and seasonal residence. Settlement on the plateau, however, increased greatly after the mid-1000s. By this time, Grand Canyon's overall population had grown significantly, and the Walhalla Plateau was one of many areas being farmed. The North Rim, at an altitude of over eight thousand feet, experienced severe winters with large snow accumulations providing ground moisture for a late spring planting. The growing seasons on the rim were short, and when cool weather arrived, the Anasazi returned to their Colorado River home sites to plant fall crops and spend the winter.

The first written report on Grand Canyon archaeology was made by John Wesley Powell on his famous expedition down the Colorado in 1869, and one of the sites he described and named, Bright Angel Pueblo, was excavated by the School of American Research on the centennial of its discovery. This ruin, situated adjacent to the Kaibab Trail about one hundred yards from the north end of the footbridge over the Colorado River, may be

visited by anyone willing to take on the arduous hike from either rim.

The Bright Angel people built a pithouse here about 1050 but were forced away by drought fifteen years later. Around 1100, the site was reoccupied, and a small above-ground pueblo was built. Its inhabitants, probably three or four families numbering about fifteen people, raised corn, beans, and squash on the small delta, gathered native plants, hunted game ranging from squirrels to bighorn sheep, and carried on seasonal maintenance chores on their pueblo. They were able to sustain themselves in this manner until around 1140, when they joined most other Grand Canyon Anasazi in a general departure from the region.

Hikers and muleback riders can view the stabilized remains of several rooms and a kiva. Trail distances from the South Rim by way of the Kaibab or Bright Angel trails are seven and nine miles, respectively; it is a fourteen-mile hike from the North Rim. Camping and overnight accommodations are available at nearby Phantom

Ranch, which also has a snack bar and restaurant.

No commentary on Grand Canyon's prehistory should omit mention of the Havasupai Indians, who have lived in the western section of the canyon along Havasu Creek for untold generations. Their home village of Supai can be visited on foot over an eight-mile trail. In prehistoric and early historic times, Havasupai life in the canyon and on the South Rim resembled that of the Anasazi centuries before. Today they lead a simple life in a beautiful valley in the last American community to receive mail delivery by mule train.

The Grand Canyon of the Colorado is one of the world's great natural wonders, a geological and scenic phenomenon of immense magnitude. It is only in recent decades, however, that the region's human prehistory has been closely studied. This lag in research has been due partly to an understandable focus on natural history and partly to the formidable environmental obstacles that are presented to even the most ardent and well-equipped archaeologist. Excavation crews at Unkar Delta in the late 1960s depended on helicopters for food and supplies. They worked for long periods in virtual isolation from the rest of the world in an area that afforded no natural shelter from high winds and where daytime temperatures often reached 120 degrees. Under such conditions, it is no wonder that archaeology in the Grand Canyon lagged behind that of other parts of the Southwest.

Suggested reading: *A Sketch of Grand Canyon Prehistory,* by Anne Trinkle Jones and Robert C. Euler. The Grand Canyon Natural History Association, 1980.
Archaeology of the Grand Canyon: The Bright Angel Site, by Douglas W. Schwartz, Michael P. Marshall, and Jane Kepp. School of American Research Press, Santa Fe, 1979.

Grand Gulch

Grand Gulch is a Primitive Area in southeastern Utah extending from the San Juan River at its south end almost to Interstate 95 at the north. The area is closed to all vehicular traffic. It can be entered from the Kane Gulch Ranger Station located off Utah 261 about 6 miles south of I-95. Permits are issued here.

Grand Gulch is a beautiful and archaeologically rich Primitive Area that is visited only by relatively few people with the time, energy, and experience to travel long distances on foot or horseback over rugged terrain.

One of the early explorers of Grand Gulch was Richard Wetherill, who led expeditions into the area in 1893–94 and again in 1896–97. Wetherill and his brothers were cattle ranchers from Mancos, Colorado, but are best remembered for their discovery of the Mesa Verde cliff dwellings. The Wetherill party cleaned out many of Grand Gulch's prehistoric cliff dwellings and sent vast quantities of artifacts to interested museums in the East and in Europe. It was at Grand Gulch that Richard came to the realization that the Pueblo culture had been preceded by an earlier culture that he termed "basketpeople"; his theory, however, which he based on stratigraphy, was not accepted by the anthropological community for many years.

Basketmaker people were very active in Grand Gulch, and their habitations and rock art are found throughout the area. Since their pithouses were semisubterranean and constructed largely of perishable materials, they are much less in evidence today than the many later Pueblo houses. Grand Gulch continued to be occupied by Anasazi until the late thirteenth century. Its inhabitants

Pueblo ruins in Grand Gulch. Photograph by Polly Schaafsma.

were culturally associated with the middle San Juan region, including Mesa Verde and the Kayenta district. Like all Anasazi, they were dry land farmers who practiced primitive irrigation methods in arable sections of the canyon and also subsisted by hunting and gathering.

One highly visible clue to Grand Gulch's prehistoric life is the great quantity and variety of rock art here, especially from the Basketmaker period. Much of this art is in the form of paintings and resembles examples found to the south in Canyon de Chelly. These sites must be found by personal exploration, for although numerous, they are scattered over many square miles and are not recorded in any hiker's guide. In contrast to architectural structures, rock art often conveys a feeling of the spiritual and religious concerns of these long disappeared people. In Grand Gulch, one can see powerful anthropomorphic and shamanistic figures as well as important items of survival such as deer, corn, and other figures that probably had symbolic content unknown to present-day observers.

Grand Gulch is administered by the Bureau of Land Management. Persons entering the area should carefully plan their trips and bring all needed supplies, for this region, in addition to being highly scenic, is a bad place to be caught without water, food, or medical requirements. Bearing in mind that Grand Gulch is a rare archaeological preserve, visitors should take care to preserve it as a continuing, undisturbed museum in nature. The gulch is regularly patrolled by BLM rangers whose duties include safeguarding the ruins and the environment.

Rock painting in Grand Gulch. Photograph by Polly Schaafsma.

Canyon de Chelly National Monument

Canyon de Chelly National Monument is located just off State 63, next to Chinle, Arizona. Chinle is reached by driving 65 miles south from U.S. 160, or 33 miles north from U.S. 264. Driving distances from Gallup and Shiprock, New Mexico, are 95 and 125 miles, respectively.

Viewed from its rim, Canyon de Chelly (shaye) one thousand feet below seems a fertile cradle of life neatly carved through the colorful sandstone formations of northern Arizona's plateau country. On the canyon floor, a glistening thread of water can usually be seen meandering along a much wider riverbed past Navajo hogans, orchards, and fields. In spring, the Rio de Chelly, which rises near the Chuska Mountains along the Arizona– New Mexico border, is full, and after heavy rains it becomes a dangerous torrent.

Canyon de Chelly, and Canyon del Muerto, which joins it, have given shelter and sustenance to human beings for over two millenia, perhaps longer. Both canyons are best known, however, for their beautiful scenery and dramatic cliff dwellings built between approximately A.D. 1050 and 1300. White House Ruins, Antelope House Ruins, Standing Cow Ruins, Sliding Rock Ruins, Junction Ruins, and Mummy Cave are some of the more familiar archaeological names. The area is also famous for its wealth of Anasazi and Navajo rock art, panels of which can be viewed on the sheer cliffs.

A few of the canyons' first residents—identified as Basketmaker people—moved in around the beginning of the Christian era. These early occupants, who had not as yet developed a knowledge of pottery making, hunting with bow and arrow, or cotton weaving, practiced primitive horticulture along with hunting and gathering. Their pithouses have often been difficult to locate due to their being buried under the layers of later occupations. Excavations at such sites as Mummy Cave, Big Cave, and Battle Cove, however, have given archaeologists a rough picture of Basketmaker life here. The presence of water, natural rock shelters, and arable land made up an environment in which population increased and settlements spread up both canyons.

The Pueblo period, which began around A.D. 700, was characterized by above-ground masonry houses, a more varied craft production, increasingly effective farming methods, and an elaborate socio-religious organization. Population in the canyons increased slowly until the thirteenth century, when many refugees from areas to the north, such as Tsegi Canyon (Navajo National Monument) and Mesa Verde, moved in. These incoming groups built larger compact cliff dwellings but stayed for only a brief period before moving on south to the region of the Hopi Mesas. The migrations in and out of Canyon de Chelly and Canyon del Muerto during the twelve hundreds reflect the generally chaotic nature of Pueblo life in the San Juan region. By A.D. 1300, Canyon de Chelly was completely or nearly abandoned.

Unlike Mesa Verde and Tsegi Canyon, however, Canyon de Chelly did not lie still and silent until discovery by Europeans. Indeed, a few families may have remained here through the Great Drought and afterwards. The canyons were certainly visited by the Hopis after A.D. 1300, and these Indians probably established summer residences and in some cases may have stayed year-round. Their presence, whatever its extent may have been, is indicated by ceramic remains and rock art and by legends passed down by word of mouth to present times. Hopi stories also tell of a northern Rio Grande Pueblo clan that migrated to Canyon de Chelly in the 1690s and remained for a brief period before joining the Hopis.

Navajos, originally a branch of the Apaches and still recognizably Apachean, moved into the Southwest from the Great Plains in the fifteenth and sixteenth centuries. Their settlement of Canyon de Chelly beginning around 1700 may have been the reason for diminished use of the area by the Hopi. During the post-Pueblo Revolt period, however, Navajo groups joined with refugee Pueblo Indians in a movement west, and much cultural exchange took place.

As the Rio Grande Valley became colonized by the Spanish and later fell under the authority of Mexico and then the United States, Canyon de Chelly developed into a Navajo stronghold. (The word *chelly* is a Spanish corruption of the Navajo word *tsegi*, meaning canyon.) In 1805, a punitive expedition under Lieutenant Antonio Narbonna encountered a band of Navajos in Canyon del Muerto where they fought an all-day battle. The rock shelter where 115 Navajos were killed is known as Massacre Cave. One of the last military conflicts between Navajo and Anglo occurred in 1864 when Kit Carson led a detachment of cavalry into Canyon de Chelly, overwhelming its Navajo forces. At this time, over eight thousand Navajos from Arizona and New Mexico were forcibly moved to Fort Sumner in eastern New Mexico, where they remained in captivity for several years before being marched back to their homeland. Approximately three hundred Navajos now live in Canyon de Chelly and Canyon del Muerto

Right: White House Ruin
Canyon de Chelly National Monument

70

Basketmaker rock paintings, Canyon del Muerto, Canyon de Chelly National Monument. Courtesy of the School of American Research. Photograph by Karl Kernberger.

from May to October, when they farm and keep flocks of sheep. Some of their hogans and corrals can be spotted from the rim.

Visitors to Canyon de Chelly can follow a twenty-two-mile Rim Drive and stop at a series of overlooks with scenic views of the canyons and of the ruins. From White House Overlook, just over six miles from monument headquarters, a two-and-a-half-mile round trip hiking trail leads to the White House Ruins, the home of about one hundred Anasazi Indians from circa A.D. 1060 to 1275. This hike, which involves climbing five hundred feet in and out of the canyon and wading across Tsegi Creek, takes one and a half to two hours. It is the only excursion to ruins in the canyon that visitors can make on their own.

People wishing to enter the canyons for a better look at archaeological sites can do so in the company of a guide, either by hiking or in their own four-wheel drive vehicle. When weather conditions permit, Thunderbird Lodge, located near the visitor center, offers half and full day commercial trips up the canyons in special open vehicles. Arrangements to hire a Navajo guide should be made in advance through monument officials. Inner canyon trips, whether on foot, commercial tour, or jeep, are beautiful and a fascinating anthropological experience. One will see many striking cliff dwellings framed by the sheer, colorful sandstone cliffs and numerous panels of Basketmaker, Pueblo, and Navajo rock art in which paintings greatly outnumber carvings. This evidence of the distant past is set against pastoral scenes of contemporary Indian life.

Facilities at the monument include a visitor center, picnic sites, and campground. Overnight accommodations and a cafeteria are available at Thunderbird Lodge, and other travel services can be found in Chinle. Three Turkey Ruins, a well-preserved cliff dwelling, can be seen from an overlook at a Navajo tribal park located a short distance beyond the monument's Spider Rock Overlook. Other interesting places to visit in the vicinity are the Hubbell Trading Post and the Hopi Mesas.

Suggested reading: *Canyon de Chelly: Its People and Rock Art,* by Campbell Grant. University of Arizona Press. 1978.
Tse Yaa Kin: House Beneath the Rock, School of American Research, Santa Fe, 1986.

Kin-Li-Chee Tribal Park

Kin-Li-Chee Tribal Park is located in northeastern Arizona 8 miles east of Ganado on State 264. A prominent sign indicates the turnoff to the park and ruins, which are situated 1.5 miles north of the highway along an unpaved road.

Kin-Li-Chee is an Anasazi pueblo ruin situated on rugged open ground overlooking Cross Canyon on the Navajo Reservation. To the north lies Canyon de Chelly; to the south, the Petrified Forest; to the east, Window Rock, capital of the Navajo Nation; to the west, the three mesas of the Hopi Indians. Kin-Li-Chee, a settlement dating from circa A.D. 800 to 1300, lies in the heartland of both the prehistoric and present-day Indian worlds. Visiting these ruins, it is hard to miss a sense of the continuity of Native American culture existing in the Southwest.

At the park one follows a rustic path between a reconstructed kiva and block of rooms, past a series of ruins marked by low masonry room walls, and on to a large excavated pueblo site protected by a modern shed roof. As of 1980, deterioration of this roof had resulted in heavy erosion of the rooms beneath. Kin-Li-Chee has undergone archaeological excavation, but little information on the site is offered at the park, and no published literature is available.

Kin-Li-Chee's main roomblock sits at the edge of a bluff overlooking a stream and valley with several Navajo farmsteads. This view from the ruins is itself worth the short detour off the highway. The site has picnic tables but no drinking water or campground. A rustic camping area, however, is located several miles east of the Kin-Li-Chee turnoff along Route 264. Restaurants and overnight accommodations can be found along Route 264 at Window Rock and at Keams Canyon. From these ruins, it is an easy drive to Hubbell Trading Post Historic Site in Ganado and to Canyon de Chelly National Monument (see p. 69), one of the loveliest scenic and archaeological areas in the region.

Kinishba Ruins

Kinishba Ruins are located just off Highway 73 about 15 miles west of Whiteriver, Arizona, between Springerville and Globe.

Like so many important archaeological sites in the Southwest, Kinishba was first reported in the early 1880s by the anthropological explorer and scholar, Adolph F. Bandelier. Half a century later, after much pothunting activity at the site by soldiers from nearby Fort Apache, a large portion of Kinishba was excavated and restored by a crew of University of Arizona students and Apache Indians under the supervision of Byron Cummings. Much of the original pueblo, however, never having experienced the archaeologist's shovel or trowel, is still seen today as overgrown mounds.

Cummings selected Kinishba for excavation because it represented, in his own words, "the highest development of the Pueblo culture." These villagers were farmers who utilized arable lands sloping southeast to the White River for the cultivation of corn, beans, and squash. Tree-ring samples date the site from the mid-eleventh through mid-fourteenth centuries, a period when Anasazi culture was vigorous and expansive. A wealth of artifacts collected during nine summers of field work bear witness to the highly developed craft skills

of these people. This collection also demonstrates the heterogeneous character of Kinishba's culture and strongly indicates that the site's inhabitants exchanged ideas and trade goods with Kayenta Anasazi peoples to the north, Tularosa people to the east, the Hopi villages of Sikyatki and Awatavi, and Salado and Hohokam communities of the lower Salt and Gila drainages to the south.

Kinishba was a large masonry pueblo consisting of several substantial community houses; one was the focus of the 1930s project. The pueblo was constructed on top of an older collapsed village, and an even older Basketmaker occupation in the area is evidenced by the presence of numerous pithouse sites. Prehistoric southwestern peoples had a propensity for reoccupying previously inhabited sites, often building new homes on top of older structures. Kinishba roomblocks were well built and compact. The excavated wing had over two hundred rooms, and the entire pueblo is believed to have held a population of fifteen hundred to two thousand people. Cummings was of the opinion that this large, productive, long-lived village must have had strong social organization and effective leadership.

At the end of Cummings's scientific investigations at Kinishba, he built a research and exhibition complex that he envisioned becoming the core of a model educational park. He hoped that in time professional and lay people would come here to tour the ruins, relax under shade trees in a park, view Kinishba art and artifacts in a modern museum, and enjoy a contemporary Native American craft center. World War II, however, shifted funding priorities away from projects like this, and public interest drifted away from Cummings's scheme. Today, Kinishba is fenced off, deteriorating, barely known to the public, and visited by few. To the serious archaeology student, however, it represents an important example of western Pueblo culture and is far from forgotten.

No services or travel facilities are offered at Kinishba Ruins, which are administered by the Fort Apache Tribe. Other archaeological sites in the general area include Besh Ba Gowah, a Salado pueblo in Globe (see p. 116), the cliff dwellings of Tonto National Monument (p. 113), and the pueblo and petroglyph sites of Petrified Forest National Park (p. 75).

Petrified Forest National Park

Petrified Forest National Park is located along Interstate 40, about 25 miles east of Holbrook, Arizona, and also along U.S. 180, about 19 miles east of Holbrook.

Petrified Forest, in central-eastern Arizona, has the largest and most colorful collection of fossilized trees in the world. Here one can walk through a series of desert "forests" where giant agate logs scatter the surface of the ground, relics of an age antedating by millions of years the presence of man in the Southwest. This desolate region, whose beauty lies in the rich colorations of its arid sands and clays, does not seem to have ever had the necessities for sustaining human life. But on its mesas and around ancient springs and seeps, many small Basketmaker and Pueblo villages, as well as abundant, fine examples of prehistoric rock art, have been found.

The earliest sites in and around the Petrified Forest belong to pithouse dwellers and date from around A.D. 500. These structures were shallow, slab-lined excavations with domelike roofs of sticks, brush, and mud, supported by poles. Two differing styles

of pottery have been associated with them—a polished brownware thought to be of Mogollon origin and a crude light-gray type identifed as Basketmaker. The presence of these two ceramic styles suggests that the region was settled by two groups of people, coming from the south and north. This area later became dotted with small pueblos inhabited by Anasazi who dry-farmed any arable corners of the landscape they could find. Over a hundred such settlements have been located in the course of archaeological surveys, suggesting that a fairly large overall population was involved.

In the fourteenth century, the small communities in the Petrified Forest area consolidated into a few substantially larger pueblos. One of these, the 125-room Puerco Ruin, occupied from the early period on into the 1300s, lies adjacent to the park's main thoroughfare and can easily be visited today. It was built in the form of a rectangle, 230 by 180 feet, surrounding a central plaza. Another easily accessible ruin is Agate House, situated at the southern end of the park. Reconstructed in 1934, this small pueblo was built of chunks of petrified wood.

Perhaps the most visually interesting evidence of prehistoric occupation at Petrified Forest is its many petroglyphs. Newspaper Rock is close to the road, and other examples can be seen at the Puerco Ruin and along the base of the mesa just south of the Rio Puerco. The Petrified Forest rock art includes a variety of geometric designs, phallic symbols, natural figures such as people and birds, animals and footprints, and intricate patterns of dots and lines. One well-known petroglyph depicts a mountain lion; another, a heron eating a frog.

Imported pottery at Petrified Forest sites indicates trade with the Hopis, Zunis, and residents of the White Mountains to the south. When the region was abandoned in the fourteenth century, these people are thought to

Petroglyphs, Petrified Forest National Park. Photograph by Polly Schaafsma.

have joined the Hopis and Zunis, whose lands lay to the north and east, respectively.

Petrified Forest was first reported in 1851 by Lieutenant Lorenzo Sitgreaves while on a U.S. Army exploratory expedition in northern Arizona. Six years later, the region was traversed by Lieutenant Beale's legendary camel caravan en route to California. After the building of the railroad in the 1880s, this bleak country saw an influx of tourists, souvenir hunters, and gem collectors. When a stamp mill was set up nearby to crush petrified logs into abrasives, public alarm was such that in 1906, President Theodore Roosevelt declared Petrified Forest a national monument.

To obtain more detailed information on Petrified Forest, its geology and prehistory, visitors should stop at the visitor center and museum. The road through the park passes near most of the more interesting fossil wood and archaeological sites.

Chaco Canyon *

Chaco Canyon is located along New Mexico 57 between Farmington and Grants. To reach the monument from the north, turn off New Mexico 44 at Blanco Trading Post and follow 57 for 23 miles to the monument's north entrance. The visitor center is 7 miles further.

From the south, turn on 57 from U. S. 66 (I-40) at Thoreau and proceed 64 miles to the south entrance. Since New Mexico 57 is unpaved between Blanco and Crownpoint, one should inquire locally regarding road conditions in wet weather.

Bumping slowly along the dusty road from Blanco Trading Post or Crownpoint to that irregular rectangle on the map marked Chaco Canyon, one may well wonder how any human habitation,

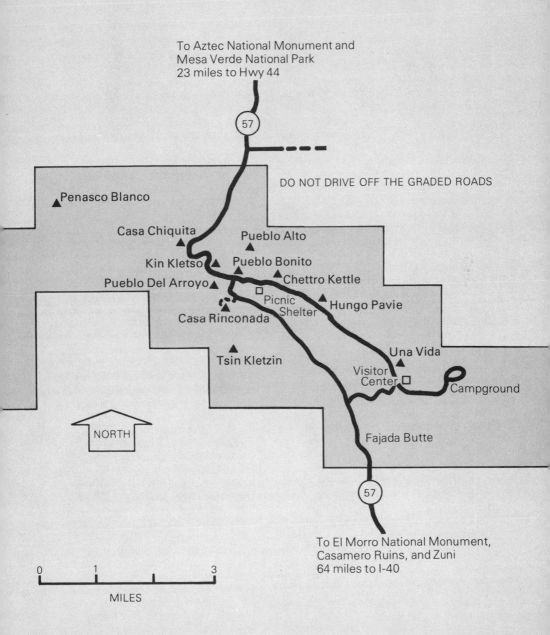

To Aztec National Monument and
Mesa Verde National Park
23 miles to Hwy 44

(57)

DO NOT DRIVE OFF THE GRADED ROADS

▲ Penasco Blanco

Casa Chiquita ▲

Kin Kletso ▲ ▲ Pueblo Alto

Pueblo Bonito ▲

Pueblo Del Arroyo ▲ ▲ Chettro Kettle

□ Picnic
Shelter ▲ Hungo Pavie

Casa Rinconada

▲ Tsin Kletzin

▲ Una Vida

Visitor
Center □

Campground

NORTH

Fajada Butte

(57)

To El Morro National Monument,
Casamero Ruins, and Zuni
64 miles to I-40

0   1   3

MILES

Chaco Canyon*

*This area has recently been designated Chaco Culture National Historical Park past or present, could lie ahead. This is a broad, rough, scrubby landscape broken only by dry washes, rock out-croppings, and distant mesas. Tire tracks occasionally branch off to points unknown. And Navajo hogans, with a wisp of wood smoke or parked pickup truck to show human presence, can sometimes be spotted. The earth here has little capacity to absorb summer rains, which run down deepening arroyos to sink eventually into the sand.

Finally one enters Chaco Canyon, a shallow rift fifteen miles long and about a mile wide, bordered on the north and south by long mesa cliffs. A series of large multistoried masonry pueblos are strung along the deeply eroded Chaco Wash, some excavated, others still mounds. As ruins, they seem to fulfill the inhospitable message of the surrounding arid environment, but as ruins they also are proof of a once teeming life in the canyon. Here was an Anasazi cultural center with a population in the thousands and a sphere of influence extending up to a hundred miles in all directions. It is little wonder that what happened along the Chaco Wash 900 years ago is commonly called "the Chaco phenomenon."

Chaco Canyon has been the subject of archaeological investigation for nearly a century. A recent survey of thirty-two square miles in and around the canyon recorded over two thousand sites. The monument itself, containing eleven large pueblos and more than four hundred smaller ruins, represents one of the richest archaeological locales in North America, a place where, in the eleventh century, one would have witnessed an apex expression of southwestern Indian culture.

The first scientific excavations here were done by the Hyde Exploring Expedition at Pueblo Bonito between 1896 and 1899. Since then, research has been sponsored by the School of American Research, University of New Mexico, National Geographic Society, Smithsonian Institution, and Natonal Park Service. In 1980, a five-year project that included extensive surveys of sites, mapping of outlying roads, excavations at Pueblo Alto, an ecological study, and investigation of farming areas was completed. And yet, despite all the years of scientific work, many basic questions surrounding Chacoan prehistory still remain topics of debate and speculation.

Humans first entered this area nine to ten thousand years ago. They were nomadic big game hunters who left a record of their passing in the form of a few stone spear points several miles to the north. About four thousand years later, Archaic hunters and gatherers were using the canyon, finding shelter several miles west of Casa Chiquita in Atlatl Cave. The cave was named for an atlatl or spear-throwing device recovered in its deposits. The next significant date relating to human occupation of the canyon is 950 to 910 B.C. when, again in Atlatl Cave, there is evidence of very early Basketmaker occupation. Other Basketmaker sites, Shabik'eshchee Village being the best known, have been found at Chaco. They span many centuries of occupation and lead up to the appearance, around A.D. 700, of small, one-storied masonry pueblos foreshadowing the great towns that made the canyon famous.

By around A.D. 900, population in the canyon was on the increase, and construction of larger, more compact pueblos had been started. A group of settlers were occupying a curved row of rooms near the north wall of the canyon, the first section of what would become the spectacular Pueblo Bonito. But the main building boom at Chaco did not get under way until about 1030 when work must have accelerated to a frenzied pace. During this century and continuing midway through the next, Chacoan culture reached its peak, making the canyon, to use contemporary terminology, the "capital" of the Anasazi world. Popu-

Bonito-style banded masonry, Chaco Canyon

Aerial view of Pueblo Bonito, Chaco Canyon. Courtesy of the National Park Service. Photograph by Fred E. Mang, Jr.

lation here grew to an estimated five thousand people, and the pueblos, with their magnificent architecture and richly decorative masonry, were a gravitational point for a far-reaching political, economic, and religious district.

There is more to be said about Chaco Canyon than could ever be summarized in a guidebook, but much information can be found in readily available publications, both popular and scientific. Archaeological research has been conducted in a number of specialized areas. The first that one might mention is architecture, for here at Chaco the highest achievements of the Anasazi as builders are on display. The name Pueblo Bonito is nearly synonymous with Chaco Canyon, and if it were necessary to pick only one site to visit, Bonito, with its 800 rooms and many kivas, should be it. And while at Bonito, one should walk next door to Kin Kletso to see a ruin of later occupation built by immigrants from

Mesa Verde. How Bonito, Chettro Kettle, Pueblo del Arroyo, Hungo Pavi, and the other great Chaco Canyon towns were built—where materials came from, how they were transported, who provided the labor—has been a major question of past research. Other areas of investigation include social organization, local, regional, and foreign trade, food resources, religion and the function of great kivas, road networks and outlying communities, agriculture and water control systems, and population movements. One recent subject of study has been astro-archaeology, particularly as it relates to the orientation of certain architectural features and to a petroglyph on Fajada Butte that is thought to have served as a seasonal calendar. The list of subjects one could investigate here seems endless. As one researcher put it, "The whole system staggers the imagination."

There are eleven major ruins in Chaco Canyon, and eight can be

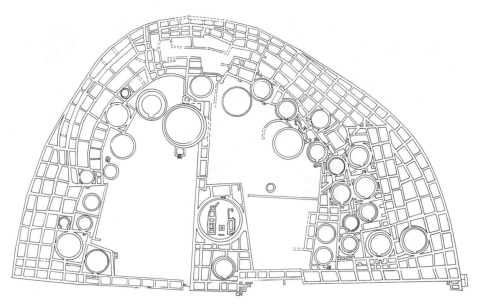

Site plan of Pueblo Bonito, Courtesy of James E. Mount

reached by road. Penasco Blanco, Tsin Kletsin, and Pueblo Alto require some hiking and climbing. In addition to the canyon ruins, four outlying towns— Kin Klezhin, Kin Bineola, Kin Ya'a, and Pueblo Pintado— are under the monument's protection. Since most of these outliers are difficult to find and some are accessible only by crossing private property, persons wishing to visit them should first consult with monument officials.

How should Chaco Canyon ruins be seen? This is largely a matter of individual preference. They can be superficially appreciated by brief, unguided visits. One can enjoy a fuller experience by using the interpretive brochures and self-guiding trails available at Pueblo Bonito, Chettro Kettle, and Casa Rinconada. This can be done at any time of day. Walks along the canyon rims offer excellent views of the entire area. Park Service rangers conduct guided tours of particular sites; a daily schedule is posted at the visitor center. Rangers also hold campfire talks at the campground to

discuss special topics relating to the area's antiquity and natural history. The visitor center has cultural and historical exhibits, literature to read, an information desk, and a fresh water tap.

In general, one would be well advised not to make too quick of a trip to Chaco Canyon. The road to the monument is long and rough and, having arrived, one finds much to see and learn. Drivers should bear in mind that once off the highway, there are no gas stations, restaurants, motels, grocery stores, or medical facilities. The canyon can be very hot in summer and equally cold in winter. Spring and fall are the best times to come here. The monument maintains a large campground at the base of scenic cliffs. Farmington and Aztec are the nearest sources of motels.

Suggested reading: *New Light On Chaco Canyon*, edited by David Grant Noble. School of American Research, Santa Fe, 1984.

West wing, Aztec Ruins National Monument

Aztec Ruins National Monument

Aztec Ruins National Monument is located just off U.S. 550 in Aztec, New Mexico, about 14 miles north of Farmington. Travelers from the east should take State 44 north from Bloomfield to Aztec, then proceed to the monument at the west edge of town.

We entered the room through the hole in the floor and passed through the open doorway into the northwest room. We broke a hole through the wall and entered the room to the northeast, and there we really did see things! I got into that room and stood, trying my best to take it all in and see everything I could, while that excited crowd were rummaging it, scattering and turning everything into a mess. There were thirteen skeletons ranging from infants to adults. ... There were several baskets, some of the best that I have ever seen, all well preserved. There were a lot of sandals, some very good, others showing considerable wear. There was a large quantity of pottery, all Mesa Verde. Some of the pottery was very pretty and new looking. There were a great many beads and ornaments. I cannot give a description of these, as I had no opportunity to examine them closely. I remember seeing quite a lot of turquoise....

When we had finished this work, the stuff was taken out and carried off by different members of the party, but where is it now? Nobody knows. Like most of the material from the smaller pueblos around the larger buildings, it is gone. I, being only a small kid, did not get my choice of artifacts. I had to take what was left, which made a nice little collection, at that. But it, too, is about all gone.

Sherman S. Howe, 1947

Sealed tombs and buried treasure contain a romance and mystery separate from but closely allied with the science of archaeology. Not a few archaeologists have a pothunting demon caged in their souls. Earl H. Morris, who devoted much of his professional life to excavating and restoring Aztec Ruins, admitted to digging up his first pot at age three and a half, "the clinching event that was to make me an ardent pot hunter, who later on was to acquire the more creditable, and I hope earned classification as an archaeologist."

Whatever their subconscious affinities may be, the pothunter and archaeologist usually are in an adversary relationship, for the success of either one precludes that of the other. Unfortunately, it is the scientist who often arrives too late. By the time Morris began work at Aztec under the auspices of the American Museum of Natural History, the site had been looted time and time again, its artifacts scattered among homes throughout the area, given away, sold, lost, or destroyed. Such a large, well-preserved pueblo must have yielded a veritable treasure trove. And yet, its very size, combined with the inaccessibility of many rooms, saved much for science.

Morris's findings quickly led him to the conclusion that Aztec had experienced two separate occupations by apparently different Anasazi groups. His excavations closest to the surface brought to light artifacts closely resembling those of Mesa Verde forty miles northwest. Under this stratum lay what archaeologists term *sterile fill,* windblown dirt containing no cultural material and indicating a period of abandonment. But beneath the fill, the excavators found more artifacts, this time bearing the stamp of Chaco Canyon fifty miles to the south. Morris's deduction was that Aztec, originally built by people associated with Chaco Canyon, had been abandoned for a period of years, later to be reoccupied by Mesa Verdeans.* The

---

*A prehistoric road, still visible today, connects Aztec Ruins with Chaco Canyon.

83

Great Kiva at Aztec Ruins

Aztec ruins

Mesa Verde occupants had cleaned out and renovated some of the earlier habitations and added rooms of their own. Tree-ring dates, obtained after Morris had completed his research, confirmed his conclusions: the Chacoan period was dated to the early twelfth century and the Mesa Verdean occupation from about 1225 to the late 1200s.

Two outstanding features will be of special interest to visitors. The reconstructed west wing of the pueblo appears today in nearly its original condition with walls, ceilings, and architectural details remarkably intact. One can enter a series of rooms gaining a sense of how it must have been to reside here eight hundred years ago. Aztec is also famous for its great kiva, which Morris reconstructed in 1934. Its large interior space is broken only by massive masonry and wood columns that support a roof estimated originally to have weighed over ninety tons. The Anasazi, like many of their Pueblo descendents, were elaborately religious people, and at Aztec's great kiva, one can gain a vivid impression of the Anasazi ceremonial environment in its fullest expression. Twenty-

nine other kivas, incidently, are situated in the pueblo.

The question of why Aztec was abandoned by its Chacoan inhabitants rests unanswered; Chaco Canyon itself, with its dozen major pueblos, was also abandoned at this time. As for the Mesa Verde reoccupation, it coincided with considerable movements of people in the Mesa Verde and Hovenweep areas and though intensive, was short-lived. The final abandonment of Aztec was only a small part of a much more widespread population exodus from the San Juan River region.

Aztec National Monument has a small interpretive museum with good displays of Pueblo artifacts, and a short audiovisual program on the natural history and prehistory of the area. Eight unexcavated sites also lie within the monument's boundaries. Another interesting feature at Aztec is the tri-walled structure known as the Hubbard Ruin situated just north of the pueblo. Its original function, thought to be ceremonial, is not well understood. Aztec Ruins is a large, well-preserved, carefully interpreted, and easily accessible site. For these reasons, and because of its archaeological importance, it has many visitors, especially in summer. The entire complex can be viewed superficially in less than an hour, but many visitors will choose to spend more time here, absorbing information made available along the trail.

Numerous travel services and facilities, including restaurants, motels, and camping areas, are located near the monument. The Salmon Ruins (see below), a contemporaneous site, are only about twelve miles away, and some people, after seeing these two noted Chacoan outliers, will no doubt be inspired to visit Chaco Canyon itself.

Salmon Ruins

The Salmon Ruins are located on the south side of U.S. 64 between Bloomfield and Farmington, New Mexico.

One of the most recently excavated prehistoric pueblos in the Southwest is the Salmon Ruins, named after Peter Milton Salmon, a Mormon homesteader who settled near the site in 1877. This large, multistoried pueblo is located on an alluvial terrace above the floodplain of the San Juan River. Excavations conducted in the 1970s by Cynthia Irwin-Williams, from Eastern New Mexico University, with a large crew of archaeologists, students, and volunteers, took place about nine hundred years after the initial building of the pueblo.

Around A.D. 1088, Chacoan people settled at this site and, using quarried sandstone blocks and timbers that were probably floated downriver from areas in southwestern Colorado, began construction of the village.

The first occupation of Salmon lasted scarcely more than two generations. For approximately a century, Salmon Pueblo lay deserted, falling into disrepair. Then, between 1225 and 1240, a large influx of Mesa Verdean people reoccupied the pueblo, carried out extensive renovations including the addition of numerous kivas, and remained until the late 1200s when they too abandoned the site.

One has only to consider the amount of labor and the degree of architectural planning and engineering skills required to build Salmon Pueblo — not to mention nearby Aztec Pueblo and the even greater towns of Chaco Canyon — to realize how energetic and well organized this society had become by its early tenth through mid-twelfth-century florescence. It would appear, however, that whatever their cultural achievements, these farmers were subject to a very fragile natural balance, and the key element was rainfall. Environmental and economic factors in the thirteenth century caused widespread disruption and change in Anasazi society, including the abandonment of population centers such as Salmon.

The San Juan County Archaeological Research Center administers the Salmon Ruins as well as a small museum and research library on the hill overlooking the site. Local artifacts are on exhibit, and a slide presentation describing archaeological excavations is offered. At the time of this writing, a ruins stabilization project is in progress, and archaeological interpretation at the ruins is being planned. The most impressive single feature at Salmon is its tower kiva built on a twenty-foot-high platform of specially selected rock believed to have been brought from thirty miles away.

The Salmon Ruins and accompanying museum are open to the public

Right: Salmon ruins

daily from 9:00 A.M. to 5:00 P.M. Overnight accommodations and travel services of all kinds can be found in the immediate locality. Other archaeological resources in the region, all having some prehistoric relationship to the Salmon Ruins, include the national monuments of Chaco Canyon (see p. 76), Aztec Ruins (p. 83), Mesa Verde (p. 31), and Hovenweep (p. 37).

Casamero Ruins

Casamero Ruins are located approximately 4 miles north of Prewitt, New Mexico. To reach the site from Interstate 40, take the Prewitt exit 20 miles west of Grants, drive east about 1 mile on old U.S. 66, turn north over the railroad tracks on an unpaved county road and continue 4.3 miles. At this point, the site will be clearly visible on the left, 150 yards off the road in front of a cliff with three large rock alcoves. Park on the county road and walk to the site.

A term currently in use among southwestern archaeologists is "Chacoan outlier." It appears in this guide in reference to such sites as Aztec, Salmon, Escalante, Lowry Ruins, and Village of the Great Kivas. Casamero is yet another example.

Chaco Canyon, fifty miles north, was a major center of Anasazi culture in the eleventh and twelfth centuries. The overall significance of this relatively small but densely populated area seems to grow with each decade of archaeological investigation. One recent subject of research has been the many widespread communities that were contemporaneous with the large Chaco Canyon towns, linked to

Left: Casamero ruins

them in social, religious, and economic ways and bearing similarities of architecture, planning, and artifact styles. A good number of these outlying towns were linked to the canyon by a network of roads, many that recently have been surveyed with the assistance of sophisticated aerial photographic techniques. Communities such as Casamero, though not necessarily settled by people from Chaco Canyon, were certainly under Chacoan influence.

The pueblo is situated on a grassy slope in the shadow of massive, red sandstone cliffs overlooking a broad valley. The valley was once scattered with small pueblos, single family farmsteads whose residents dry-farmed fields of corn, beans, and squash in the floodplain. Casamero, it is assumed, was the center of this dispersed community, fulfilling a role that archaeologists are only presently beginning to understand. Two hundred and forty-five feet south of the ruins there is a large circular depression in the ground, an overgrown cattle tank at first appearance, but, in reality, the remains of a great kiva. Its diameter is conservatively estimated at seventy feet, making it almost twice the size of the reconstructed great kiva at Aztec Ruins and slightly larger than the one at Casa Rinconada in Chaco Canyon. Casamero itself is a smallish pueblo, no more than thirty rooms, but the size of its great kiva suggests the former presence of a considerably large area population.

Today only Casamero's twenty-three ground-floor rooms can be seen, their walls waist or shoulder high. Anyone who has been to Pueblo Bonito and the other Classic pueblos of Chaco Canyon will recognize the characteristic banded masonry in which large sandstone blocks alternate with layers of chinking using small limestone fragments. When looking at this excellent and aesthetically pleasing craftsmanship, one should realize that these walls, when in use, were covered with mud plaster.

Casamero was excavated in 1966 and 1967 and subsequently stabilized by the Bureau of Land Management for public visitation. The pueblo was built and occupied around A.D. 1050 and used for approximately seventy years. Extensive archaeological surveying, testing, and excavation around the pueblo was carried out by the School of American Research to obtain clearance for construction of a coal-fired electrical generating plant and associated roads and railroad spur in the valley. This research brought to light the presence of over one hundred and forty archaeological sites in the vicinity, ranging from Basketmaker pithouses and Pueblo structures from the eleventh century and before to twentieth-century Navajo hogans, ramadas, sheep pens, and sweat lodges. Beginning in the summer of 1980, the quiet pastoral quality of this valley will change drastically; Casamero , overlooking gigantic boilers and smokestacks fed by trainloads of coal, will stand out as a contrasting monument to southwestern antiquity.

The Bureau of Land Management, which administers Casamero Ruins, has installed several helpful interpretive signs at the site, which can be thoroughly toured in fifteen or twenty minutes. The nearest travel services are at Milan and Grants, twenty miles east on I-40, and at Gallup, forty miles west.

Village of the Great Kivas

Village of the Great Kivas is located on the Zuni Reservation in west-central New Mexico. Zuni Pueblo, about 17 miles from the ruins, is located along New Mexico 53, 35 miles south of Gallup and 71 miles west of Grants. Persons wishing to visit this site should contact the Zuni Tribal Offices for permission and directions. The address is P. O. Box 339, Zuni, New Mexico 87327, and the phone number is (505) 782-4686.

Unlike the nearby Zuni site of Hawikuh (see p. 92), Village of the Great Kivas had long been abandoned when Europeans first penetrated the American Southwest in 1640. This site, named for two great kivas that lie just outside the pueblo walls, was one of the farthest flung outliers of Chaco Canyon, about eighty miles to the north. Its banded masonry, which echoes that of Pueblo Bonito, and its great kivas are clearly visible indications of the site's Chacoan connection during its peak development in the eleventh century.

The pueblo is situated on a slope at the foot of a mesa overlooking the broad Nutria Valley. Only a few rooms, with waist to shoulder high walls, are exposed; others, however, can be inferred by substantial earthen mounds. The great kivas appear as large circular depressions in front of the site. Although smaller and less striking, this pueblo is strongly reminiscent of Casamero (see p. 89) some thirty miles to the northeast. Village of the Great Kivas was excavated in the 1930s by Frank H. H. Roberts, an archaeologist perhaps best remembered for his excavations of Shabik'eshchee Village, a large Basketmaker site in Chaco Canyon.

Perhaps the most striking feature associated with this site is the two rock painting panels located along the cliff behind it. These paintings were executed by a Zuni Indian in the 1920s and are representations of masks and other figures that will be familiar to

Right: Village of the Great Kivas

Rock paintings near Village of the Great Kivas

persons who have witnessed Zuni ceremonial dances. To reach these panels, climb the rocky talus slope behind the site and follow the cliff to the right a short distance. One can climb onto ledges directly in front of the paintings for a close look, but great care must be taken not to touch or brush against the artwork. Unfortunately, several of the figures have already been damaged.

Village of the Great Kivas is a small site that is only partially excavated and not interpreted. For these reasons, it has more limited appeal than many ruins in this book. But for specialists, and particularly archaeologists interested in the Chacoan cultural phenomenon of the eleventh and twelfth centuries, much can be gained by seeing the site. Anyone inspired by these rock paintings should certainly make an effort to see the murals recently painted in the nave of the old mission church in Zuni.

Hawikuh

The ruins of Hawikuh are located about 12 miles south of Zuni Pueblo in western New Mexico. Zuni is located on State 53, 35 miles south of Gallup, 71 miles west of Grants. To see Hawikuh, one should obtain permission from the Zuni Tribal Office (see p. 90), which will supply a guide.

The year was 1539 when a Spanish Moor named Esteban, an advance scout for Fray Marcos de Niza, arrived at the Zuni pueblo of Hawikuh with a small group of Mexican Indians. Hawikuh was an impressive hilltop village, described by its contemporary observers as equivalent in size to Mexico City, and as Esteban made his approach, fame and fortune were probably not far from his thoughts.

Hawikuh Pueblo mounds

According to legend, he was a confident man with a touch of flamboyance and a gift for languages. Little did he suspect that within a few hours he would be dead.

According to his own account, Fray Marcos and some of his party advanced to within sight of the pueblo several days later. Perhaps the afternoon sun shone resplendently off Hawikuh's high walls. Knowing of Esteban's misfortune, the priest proceeded no further, but he was impressed; the report filed on his return to Mexico City stimulated another adventurer, Francisco Vasquez de Coronado, to organize a follow-up expedition.

After Coronado and his army successfully stormed Hawikuh in 1540, the expedition's chronicler wrote, "We found what we needed more than gold and silver, and that was much corn, and beans and turkeys...." After their arduous journey, the Spaniards

no doubt appreciated some home cooking, but at the same time, they were bitterly disappointed to discover the Zuni's lack of precious metals. After a short stay, Coronado continued to the Rio Grande.

Hawikuh saw no more Spaniards until they returned in 1629, erected a church, and established a daily presence at the pueblo. The church was burned by the Indians in 1632, rebuilt, reburned, built again, and destroyed for a final time in the Pueblo Revolt of 1680. At this time, the Zunis abandoned Hawikuh altogether.

Ceramics found at the site indicate that Hawikuh was inhabited as early as about 1300, but questions remain as to how ancient the earliest parts of the site may be. Archaeological excavations were carried out in 1922 and 1923 by Frederick Webb Hodge, but his interest was limited to the period of Spanish-Indian contact, and he left earlier levels of Hawikuh unprobed.

Unfortunately, Hodge neither back-filled nor stabilized his excavations, with the result that weathering subsequently reduced the pueblo again to rubbled mounds. The site of the ill-fated mission church, however, can be recognized, and here and there, a portion of a pueblo wall still stands. But even if these ruins are unimpressive today, the village site itself is striking by virtue of its size and commanding position. In addition, to stand upon the very spot where, four and a half centuries ago, the Spanish empire first confronted natives of the American Southwest is an experience to stir the imagination.

Hawikuh was one of the Seven (in actuality only six) Golden Cities of Cíbola. It is administered today by the Zuni Indians, who are interested in their cultural heritage and in archaeological conservation on tribal land. Preliminary plans are in the offing to develop Hawikuh into a national monument; such a project could greatly enhance public understanding of this very early historical period. To visit the site today, one should plan at least an hour and a half excursion from Zuni Pueblo. Another archaeological ruin on the Zuni reservation that can be visited with a guide is Village of the Great Kivas (see p. 90).

Cafes, grocery stores, gas stations, and a campground can be found at or near Zuni Pueblo. The nearest motels are in Gallup, along Interstate 40.

Suggested reading: *The Spanish Borderlands Frontier, 1513–1821,* by John Francis Bannon. Holt, Rinehart and Winston, 1970.
Zuni & El Morro, School of American Research, Santa Fe, 1983.

Left: Atsinna Pueblo,
El Morro National Monument

El Morro National Monument

El Morro National Monument is located on Route 53, 40 miles west of Grants and 30 miles east of Zuni, New Mexico.

The ruins of Atsinna, a thirteenth-century Zuni village fortress, are perched near the rim of El Morro Mesa with a bird's-eye view over the upper valley of the Zuni River. Below, like the prow of a great stone ship, is Inscription Rock, bearing the names and comments of conquistadores, explorers, settlers, and others known only by their signatures. At its base, a large pool collects run-off from the mesa. Forty-odd miles downstream lie the ruins of Hawikuh, principal village of the Zuni Indians in the sixteenth century and the first community in the American Southwest to experience the Spanish invasion that began in 1540.

El Morro, which means headland or bluff in Spanish, was on the route from Hawikuh to the Rio Grande and Santa Fe, the Spanish colonial capital of New Mexico. It became traditional, while stopping to take water at the pool, to inscribe one's name, the date, and sometimes a comment on the base of the rock. In time, this site became a unique folk-historical register of nearly two centuries of exploration, conquest, and settlement.

Archaeological research in the El Morro region has turned up evidence of Paleo and Archaic hunters and gatherers going back thousands of years. Further downriver toward Zuni, numerous pithouse villages dating from about A.D. 400 to 900, as well as later pueblo communities, can be found. But settlement of the El Morro valley itself did not begin until the middle 1200s. At this time, Indians from the Zuni area, confronting drought conditions, moved up to the higher elevations of El Morro to take advantage of greater precipitation. These farmers first built small, scattered, relatively defenseless pueblos throughout the valley, but after a few years, probably as a consequence of local warfare, they consolidated into densely populated, well-fortified pueblos like Pueblo de los Muertos and Atsinna. The latter's two-story exterior walls have no entrances, and from their ramparts sentries could have surveyed the entire valley, keeping watch on nearby communities. This defensive posture indicates that hostile conditions probably existed among the pueblos of the El Morro Valley.

Pueblo de los Muertos, outside the monument and not open to the public, is nearly identical to Atsinna in architectural design, a most unusual if not unique occurrence in prehistoric southwestern village planning. Each pueblo was apparently planned as a complete unit, constructed in a single building period, then occupied by its full quota of residents.

The drought that stimulated the Zuni move to El Morro, and also caused social disruptions throughout the Southwest, terminated in 1299. Soon thereafter, the occupants of Atsinna and its neighboring pueblos moved back downriver to their original territory. Very likely, they were the ancestors of the Zunis, encountered by Coronado 250 years later, residing in the Seven (actually only six) Cities of Cíbola. Their move to El Morro, lasting but two or three generations, illustrates the sensitivity of prehistoric Pueblo communities to climatic fluctuations. The Atsinna site testifies to the architectural energy and expertise of these people in the face of defense needs.

One large wing of Atsinna was excavated in the 1950s by Richard B. Woodbury and later stabilized by the National Park Service. Woodbury reported that the Atsinna inhabitants collected rainwater from natural rock basins and also from several larger reservoirs on the mesa. The pool at Inscription Rock would also have been a good water source. Further archaeological investigations here, at Pueblo de los Muertos, and throughout the area, were conducted by Steven LeBlanc, who is best known today for his work on the Mimbres culture and who was instrumental in 1979 in successfully promoting passage in Congress of a new legislative act protecting archaeological sites (see p. 155).

Atsinna is reached by means of a short, steep footpath from the visitor center. The trail passes through the site's excavated wing consisting of a dozen or more masonry rooms and two kivas. A permanent site map has been installed here to indicate the full extent of this 500- to 1000-room rectangular pueblo. Anyone who hikes up the mesa will be impressed by the views over the surrounding valley and mesas. From Atsinna, the trail continues across the mesa and on to a second undisturbed pueblo site. From here, one descends the back cliff to return along the foot of the mesa to Inscription Rock. The walk only to Atsinna and back takes up to three quarters of an hour; the full circuit requires about double this time.

El Morro is a particularly rewarding place to visit, for it combines interesting historic and prehistoric sites with beautiful natural scenery. The monument maintains an attractive, nine-unit campground and a picnic area. Its visitor center includes a small historic display, lounge, publication stand, and information desk. The nearest gas station is at Ramah, fifteen miles distant, and overnight accommodations can be found along I-40 at either Gallup or Grants. Several Forest Service camping areas are also nearby. As a follow-up to visiting El Morro, some people may be interested in seeing the contemporary Zuni Pueblo where arrangements can be made for a guided tour of Hawikuh (see p. 92) and Village of the Great Kivas (p. 90).

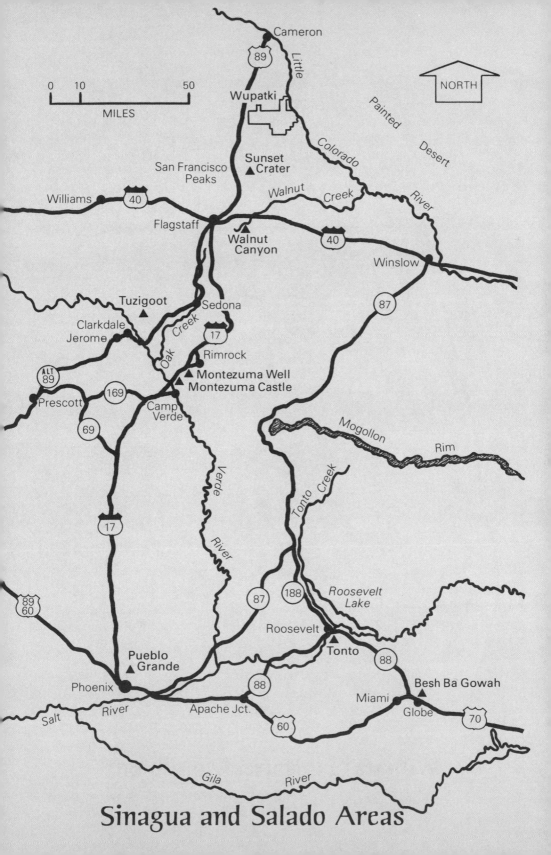

Sinagua and Salado Areas

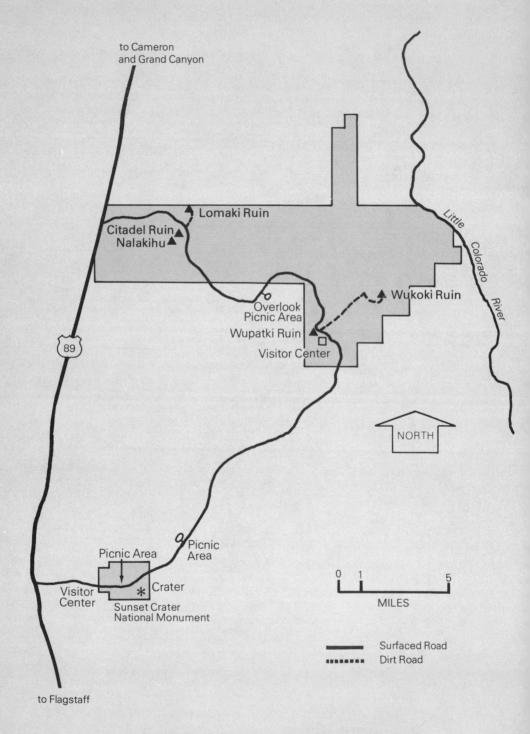

to Cameron
and Grand Canyon

Lomaki Ruin

Citadel Ruin
Nalakihu

Little

Colorado

River

89

Overlook
Picnic Area

Wupatki Ruin

Wukoki Ruin

Visitor Center

NORTH

Picnic Area

Picnic
Area

Visitor
Center

Crater

Sunset Crater
National Monument

0   1   5

MILES

Surfaced Road
Dirt Road

to Flagstaff

Wupatki National Monument

THE SINAGUA
Anasazi Frontiers

Water, the desert's most elusive natural resource, has always been the key to survival in the Southwest and has determined the quality of life for the region's inhabitants. Any map of early southwestern cultures quickly reveals the relationship between population centers and sources of water.

Despite their name (Spanish for "without water"), the Sinagua (Seen-áwa) did have water. Early in their development they discovered an unusual and effective method of farming based on water conservation; later, they learned the art of irrigation.

The first Sinagua emerged as a scattered population of pithouse dwellers in the region around present-day Flagstaff, Arizona. The introduction and local development of new strains of drought and cold resistant corn succeeded in drawing these groups to a more settled, communal, agricultural way of life. By about the eighth century A.D., these former hunter-gatherers were building pithouses, planting crops, and accumulating artifacts that archaeologists identify as early Sinagua. This culture, germinated in the shadow of the San Francisco Peaks and along the fringes of old volcanic ash fields, continued to evolve for seven centuries.

Travelers approaching Flagstaff from the east or northeast will notice a large volcanic area marked by black cinder cones. The Sinagua were intimately tied to this unusual geological phenomenon that for a brief era offered them and other neighboring peoples a solution to the difficulties of desert farming. In the Flagstaff area, at an altitude of seven thousand feet, farming is favored by abundant moisture but curtailed by a short growing season. At lower altitudes, rainfall is too much reduced. To solve this dilemma, the Sinagua cultivated corn, beans, and squash in areas of lower altitude that were covered by a thin, even layer of volcanic cinder and ash. This ground cover acted as a moisture-conserving mulch that provided nutrients to the underlying soil.

In the winter of 1064–65, an event occurred thrusting the Sinagua into the center of an economic, cultural, and population boom that lasted at least 150 years and revolutionized their way of life. A volcano, Sunset Crater, was born. The sudden tearing of the earth's skin, the fire and smoke, molten lava, thundering volcanic bombs, and high flying cinder and ash must have made a profound impression on these people, but following the trauma, the Sinagua found themselves surrounded by 800 square miles of new agricultural potential.

Word of these new farming lands spread to neighboring Indian communities, and before long the Sinagua saw the arrival of Hohokam from the south, Anasazi from the north, Cohonina from the west, and Cibola (Mogollon) peoples from the east. The unprecedented intermingling of cultures that developed was peaceful, prosperous, and mutually beneficial. Exchange of ideas and practices took place at many levels, including religion, village concepts, building techniques, recreation, and arts and crafts.

Sunset Crater. Courtesy of the National Park Service. Photograph by Fred E. Mang, Jr.

The Sinagua demonstrated a special receptivity to change. They learned surface masonry architecture from the Anasazi, and crafts, irrigation, and the ritual ball court game from the Hohokam. Sinagua culture evolved into patterns almost unrecognizable from its less sophisticated origins. The center of contact between these different cultural groups lay a few miles southwest of the Little Colorado River and north of Sunset Crater, where Wupatki National Monument is now situated. The rising population and widespread movements of peoples, however, motivated many Sinagua to move to Walnut Canyon, twenty-five miles to the south. Here they built Pueblo-style cliff dwellings in recesses along the canyon sides and dry-farmed near the rims. Still others expanded further south to the Verde Valley, establishing farming pueblos in areas recently abandoned by northbound Hohokam.

The northern Sinagua thrived for a century or more. But beginning in 1215, the Southwest experienced a marked decrease in rainfall, causing agricultural problems from which the ash-fall farmers of Wupatki and Walnut Canyon were not spared. The Anasazi withdrew to their original Kayenta homeland, and the Sinagua migrated to the more reliable water sources of the Verde Valley. Tuzigoot, Montezuma Castle, and other neighboring Hohokam and Sinagua communities grew rapidly. As the drought intensified during the late thirteenth century, the northern Sinagua lands were abandoned altogether. The Verde Valley, meanwhile, experienced a population boom that is believed to have strained the ability of the area's natural resources to support the population.

Much remains to be learned about the last years of the Sinagua. They stayed in the Verde Valley until the early fifteenth century, and why they ultimately departed is still an archaeological unknown. A prevalent theory holds that the final move of the Sinagua was to the land of the Hopi to the northeast. What is certain is that when the first Spanish explorers entered the Verde Valley in 1583, they found the pueblos of the Sinagua in ruins and the valley inhabited by Yavapai Indians living in huts with thatched roofs.

There are four major archaeological areas where visitors today can see the tangible remains of Sinagua culture. They are the national monuments of Wupatki (see below), Walnut Canyon (p. 104), Montezuma Castle (p. 107), and Tuzigoot (p. 105). All are within easy reach of Flagstaff. Wupatki, Sunset Crater, and Walnut Canyon make up a full day's tour. Tuzigoot, Montezuma Castle, and nearby Montezuma Well (see p. 111) comprise another day trip that could be extended by including time in Oak Creek Canyon and the old mining town of Jerome. The four Sinagua areas are remarkably dissimilar from one another both in architectural style and natural surroundings. This variety reflects the imaginative and adaptive nature of these early southwesterners.

Suggested reading: *Of Men and Volcanoes: The Sinagua of Northern Arizona* by Albert H. Schroeder. Southwest Parks and Monuments Association, 1977.

Wupatki National Monument

Wupatki National Monument is located 14 miles east of Arizona 89 between Flagstaff and Cameron. A 36-mile driving loop from route 89 passes through this monument and Sunset Crater National Monument.

The Wupatki Basin, which contains the ruins of Wupatki, Wukoki, Citadel, Lomaki, and numerous other pueblos and archaeological sites, is a spacious and desolate landscape. Depending on the season, one may experience temperatures from near zero to over one hundred degrees. The region's scant annual rainfall is quickly evaporated by sweeping winds, which allow only the toughest vegetation to survive. This seems a most unlikely locale to nurture a human population estimated at over four thousand.

Prior to the eruption of Sunset Crater, the Wupatki Basin was virtually uninhabited. Alluvial terraces along the Little Colorado River to the east have revealed evidence of stone tool manufacturing by Archaic peoples, and in later times, the Sinagua, who inhabited the region to the south and east of the San Francisco Peaks, no doubt used the Basin for hunting-and-gathering forays. But the region was too inhospitable to attract permanent human occupants.

The A.D. 1064–65 eruption of Sunset Crater (dated by tree-ring analysis) distributed a fine blanket of cinder and ash over a large area, including what today is Wupatki National Monument. The resulting increase in the retention of ground moisture made dry farming a feasible enterprise. The Sinagua and Cohonina peoples were the first to take advantage of this new potential but were soon followed by Anasazi from the Kayenta region. Hohokam from the Verde Valley moved up to within twenty miles of Wupatki, and Cibola peoples, with strong Mogollon connections, moved in from the east. Added to this mix indirectly were the far-reaching trade contacts of each immigrant group. Within two generations of Sunset Crater's fireworks, the Wupatki Basin had become transformed into a unique southwestern melting pot.

Wupatki Pueblo, which stands behind the monument's visitor center, was the only major pueblo in the area built and inhabited by Sinagua. Dating from as early as 1106, its sandstone masonry walls reflect the quick adoption by the Sinagua of Anasazi building methods. Adjacent to the ruins sits a large excavated "amphitheater." Although this structure bears some resemblance to Anasazi kivas, it was unroofed and lacks usual kiva ceremonial features. It is a unique structure, the purpose of which remains uncertain. Behind Wupatki is a small masonry ball court, evidence of Hohokam contact and influence. This game was introduced to the Hohokam from Mexico where, in the sixteenth century, Spanish observers indicated that it was strenuous and had religious or ritualistic overtones. Its significance and method of playing in southwestern culture, however, are not clearly known.

Wukoki, Citadel, and Lomaki ruins, all occupied by Kayenta Anasazi, are located along Wupatki's driving loop and are interesting to visit. Persons with more time and energy may obtain permission to visit other less accessible ruins such as Crack-in-Rock; arrangements, however, should be made in advance with monument officials.

The Anasazi, whose heartland was in the Four Corners region to the northeast, were a dynamic, expansive culture that was reaching its peak of influence in the twelfth century. The Kayenta, a distinctive Anasazi sub-group, lost no time in becoming the dominant cultural element in the Wupatki area. The Cohonina, who had a smaller population, continued for the most part to live in pithouses. For this reason, their cultural remains are now in little evidence.

For slightly more than a century, the multicultural life of Wupatki was carried on with apparent success. The differing communities intermingled peacefully and productively. Their life, however, was probably far from luxurious. The beneficial ash fall, combined with normal precipitation, made farming possible but never highly productive. It is noteworthy that the pueblos of the Wupatki Basin were not long-lived, with the droughts of the thirteenth century dispersing their populations as fast as they had gathered a century earlier. Other problems such as wind erosion and soil depletion from leaching are believed to have intensified Wupatki's misfortunes.

The Sinagua relocated, first in small groups and then in larger numbers, in the Verde Valley, where they found not only related Indian groups but dependable water. Except for a possible brief Hopi occupation fifty years later, the pueblos of Wupatki lay undisturbed for six centuries.

Beginning in 1851 with an exploratory expedition led by Lieutenant Lorenzo Sitgreaves, the Wupatki area was visited sporadically by explorers, scientists, and pothunters until its establishment as a national monument in 1924. Nine years later, the Museum of Northern Arizona undertook systematic excavations of Wupatki Pueblo. Although archaeological investigations of the Monument have continued up to the present day, many ruins remain unexcavated. A thorough archaeological survey of the area is scheduled for 1981.

The historic period at Wupatki has witnessed an interesting series of developments. The story of Mormon settlers, Anglo cattle ranchers, Navajo sheepherders, miners, traders, and railroad people, not to mention National Park Service personnel and tourists, would require a book in itself.

Since the prehistory of Wupatki is closely tied to nearby volcanic activities, visitors should plan also to stop at adjoining Sunset Crater National Monument. Both monuments, located off Arizona 89 northeast of Flagstaff, are clearly marked on road maps. The thirty-six-mile driving loop passes four major pueblo ruins, skirts Sunset Crater, and includes several scenic views of the

Wupatki ruins

Painted Desert and the volcanic cones. One could conceivably take this drive and see the high points in less than two hours; however, to take advantage of Wupatki's archaeological potential and also spend time at Sunset Crater would require a half-day or longer.

The visitor center at Wupatki includes a small, informative exhibit area that explains the region's history and describes its prehistoric human occupation. On display are a variety of Sinagua crafts and a typical Wupatki room reconstruction. Picnic sites are available, but the area's blustering winds may discourage this activity in the open. Sunset Crater National Monument maintains a campground from spring through fall. Travel facilities can be found along Route 89, particularly near Flagstaff and Cameron. Within an hour's drive south is Walnut Canyon National Monument (see p. 104), another center of Sinagua life in a much different natural setting.

Suggested reading: *Wupatki: An Archaeological Assessment* by Dana Hartman and Arthur H. Wolf. Museum of Northern Arizona, Flagstaff. 1977.

Walnut Canyon cave dwelling

Walnut Canyon National Monument

Walnut Canyon National Monument is located at the end of 3 miles of paved road connecting with Interstate 40 approximately 7.5 miles east of Flagstaff, Arizona.

Archaeology aside, a visit to Walnut Canyon is a memorable experience. The canyon is a veritable haven from the outside world, set aside by 400-foot rock walls. This is an environment to stimulate the geologist, naturalist, and photographer, not to mention anyone with a curiosity about the past.

Like Wupatki and the Verde Valley, Walnut Canyon was a principal center of Sinagua culture. Taking advantage of cave-like niches in the canyon walls, prehistoric Indians built many small homes here following a twelfth-century move from more crowded areas to the north. Through their contact with Anasazi peoples at Wupatki, they learned masonry skills; and from many vantage points along the monument's interpretive trail, the rock walls of residences and granaries tucked under cliff overhangs can be spotted. Small and scattered as they are throughout the canyon, these humble structures were a far cry from the great cliff dwellings of the Anasazi. But they were safe, efficient, and in tune with the surrounding environment.

Walnut Canyon in the twelfth century must have been vibrant with human life and activity. Its cliffs afforded the Sinagua shelter, and its stream provided water. Edible plants abounded, game was plentiful and farming lands lay within a two-mile walk of the rim. The Walnut Canyon Sinagua apparently lived in relative comfort and security from the early to mid-1100s until after the onset of serious droughts in the thirteenth century. Many are believed to have migrated south to the Verde Valley, becoming the inhabitants of pueblos such as Tuzigoot and Montezuma Castle.

By the time archaeologists arrived here, Walnut Canyon had been stripped by vandals and pothunters. Much of what is known of the area's prehistory comes from excavations at other similar sites of the same time period. Since 1933, this rich area has been under the protection of the National Park Service.

The visitor center includes exhibits that interpret the canyon's geologic and human history and explain how the Sinagua carried on agriculture, hunting, and trade. A fine botanical case, a display of tree rings for dating, and a diorama representing an A.D. 1150 to 1250 cliff dwelling are also of interest.

The trail loop from the visitor center through the canyon is three-quarters of a mile long, and persons planning to take the walk might note that it involves a steep two-hundred-foot ascent at an elevation of seven thousand feet. The trail passes by several cliff ruins and is highlighted by scenic views over the canyon. A published trail guide offers information on the natural environment and archaeological sites. Food, gas, lodging, and camping are not available at the monument but can be found in the Flagstaff area and along major highways.

Tuzigoot National Monument

Tuzigoot National Monument is located off Alternate 89, between Cottonwood and Clarkdale, Arizona.

Perched on a 120-foot limestone ridge, Tuzigoot Pueblo holds a commanding view over the entire upper Verde Valley and looks down on the Verde River, which loops close by the south foot of the ruins. The river nourished Tuzigoot and six other fourteenth-century pueblos in the vicinity, supporting their agricultural life and creating riparian environments that harbored many species of edible plants, game, and wildlife. The Verde flows on to become the major drainage of central Arizona.

The story of Tuzigoot goes back to at least A.D. 700, when Hohokam farming people migrated into the valley from the Gila Basin to the south. A few dwellings are believed to have existed on the ridge prior to A.D. 1000, and more were added in the early twelfth century with the arrival of Sinagua groups from the north. The real growth of the pueblo, however, took place in the mid-thirteenth century, when much larger numbers of Sinagua from the

Tuzigoot ruins

vicinity of present-day Flagstaff, having been uprooted by droughts, relocated in the Verde Valley. This same period also witnessed the concentration of the valley's population into larger, fortified pueblos close to the river. Tuzigoot's population is estimated to have quad-rupled to approximately 225 people.

Archaeologists hypothesize that the Verde Valley's population growth in the mid- to late-1200s overwhelmed the region's natural and agricultural resources, introduced threats of star-vation, disease, and warfare, and strained the social order of the

Hohokam-Sinagua communities. While the very limited archaeological work that has been conducted in the valley supports such a theory, more research needs to be accomplished before we really know what happened here seven centuries ago. What does appear clear, however, is that the inner valley communities rode out the Great Drought of 1276 to 1299 and contin-ued for another century.

The people of Tuzigoot practiced irrigation farming as their principal livelihood, with hunting and gathering to supplement this economic base.

They were strategically situated between the vital Hohokam culture near present-day Phoenix and the progressive, expansive Anasazi of Wupatki and beyond. Cohonina and Mogollon groups lay to the northwest and east, respectively. This favorable placement of the Verde Valley pueblos, combined with the existence of nearby mineral and salt deposits, helped to make Tuzigoot an active center of trade.

Why the Sinagua ultimately departed and where they went remain archaeological mysteries. A contemporary Hopi legend tells of a group of people from the south who, lacking ceremonies and priests, joined the Hopi in a previous era. If the legend refers to the Sinagua, it coincides with the picture archaeologists reconstruct of Sinagua religious life. The idea of a migration to Hopi country is also supported by similarities of pottery and basketry.

The remains of Tuzigoot were very likely seen by Antonio Espejo and his party during their exploration of the Verde Valley in 1583. Three hundred years later, mining operations were initiated at Jerome, where copper had been quarried by Indians since prehistoric times. In 1932 federal relief funds were used to conduct a two-year archaeological investigation at the pueblo. In a relatively short period, the ruins were almost entirely excavated by a force of 148 laborers under the direction of two University of Arizona graduate students. Archaeology during this era was often directed more toward the accumulation of museum collections than to careful scientific research. For this reason, much data about Tuzigoot's prehistory was unrecovered and little material left for future study. Hopefully, this information gap will be filled when other sites in the valley from the same period are excavated using modern methods.

Tuzigoot National Monument has one of the best archaeological exhibits in the Southwest. The many displays include excellent examples of prehistoric jewelry, basketry, tools, textiles, and religious objects, as well as a most interesting Pueblo room reconstruction. Visitors should plan about a half-hour to see the museum and at least the same length of time to take the trail through Tuzigoot Pueblo. The trail is easy to negotiate and offers good views up and down the Verde Valley.

Tuzigoot is located between Flagstaff and Prescott. Travelers to Tuzigoot from the north will enjoy the scenery of Oak Creek Canyon; persons coming up from Prescott will pass through the historic and picturesque mining town of Jerome. Any itinerary should include Montezuma Castle (see below), a spectacular cliff ruin twenty-seven miles east of Tuzigoot that offers a very different view of the architectural accomplishments of the Sinagua.

Suggested reading: *Tuzigoot: An Archaeological Overview,* by Dana Hartman. Museum of Northern Arizona. 1976.

Montezuma Castle National Monument

Montezuma Castle National Monument in northern Arizona is located several miles east of Interstate 17, just north of Camp Verde and less than an hour's drive south of Flagstaff. The exit from I-17 is well marked.

Montezuma, the sixteenth-century Aztec ruler, was never exiled to North America. But had such a fate befallen him, no more fitting residence could he have had than the "castle" that today bears his name. Impregnably situated on the ledges of a sheer cliff overlooking Beaver Creek in the Verde Valley, Montezuma Castle is a striking example of prehistoric Indian architecture. Its seventeen rooms reach a maximum of five stories and have been preserved as well as any ruins in the Southwest. Occupied six hundred and more years ago, the pueblo represents one of the last structures built by the Sinagua Indians.

The Sinagua, who originated as a culture in the forested plateau near present-day Flagstaff, first moved to the Verde Valley in the early twelfth century. At this time, the valley was the northernmost settlement of the Hohokam, some of whom were migrating even further north to utilize the ash-fall agricultural potential around Sunset Crater. The Sinagua settled in peacefully with the Hohokam, introducing them to masonry skills acquired from the Anasazi at Wupatki and learning irrigation in return. The Verde Valley, in addition to providing a steady water supply, offered arable bottomland, a variety of wild food plants and berries, fish and game, and the raw materials for building, tool manufacture, and ceramics. The Sinagua built small farming pueblos and carried on a peaceful, secure existence for more than a century.

Thirteenth-century droughts brought unrest to most parts of the Southwest, and the Verde Valley was not excepted. The exodus from Wupatki and Walnut Canyon brought droves of Sinagua south, causing critical social and economic problems. Although several rooms of Montezuma Castle date to the 1100s, the pueblo as it is seen today was built during these hard times, and its essentially defensive character is unmistakable.

The castle, sheltered under a deep overhang in the cliff, is constructed of small limestone blocks laid in mud mortar and roofed by large sycamore timbers overlaid by poles, sticks, grass, and several inches of mud. Observers today can imagine the effort required to haul these heavy materials up the cliff face. The outer room walls of the pueblo sit nearly at the edge of the high ledges and are curved to conform to the arc of the surrounding cave. One hundred feet below the ruin flows Beaver Creek, the life force of this prehistoric community. While remains of corn, beans, and squash in the pueblo point to the inhabitants' agricultural way of life, other plant remains, including wild seeds and nuts, indicate a continued dependency on gathering. Montezuma Castle was a fortress to its forty-five or fifty residents. Two paths, one from the valley floor that no doubt required the use of ladders, and one from along the side of the cliff, joined to enter the pueblo. At the junction of the two paths sits a small smoke-blackened room believed to have been a sentry post. Small inner keyhole doorways conserved heat and made hostile entry all but impossible.

The castle had a relatively brief occupancy. For reasons still unclear the Sinagua left the Verde Valley early in the fifteenth century. Speculations as to the reasons for abandonment include overpopulation, exhaustion of farm land, depletion of natural resources, outside attack, and internal social disintegration.

Because of their fragility, the ruins may no longer be entered. A paved pathway about a quarter mile long leads from the visitor center to an excellent view of the site, continues past some other ruins (Castle "A") at the base of the cliff, and returns along Beaver Creek. The musem at the visitor center has exhibits illustrating Sinagua life in the Verde Valley and displays some of the tools and handicrafts of these early people. Visitors should plan on spending at least a half-hour here and can expect plenty of company—the monument accommodates nearly half a million visitors each year.

Right: Montezuma Castle

Montezuma Well

Montezuma Well

Montezuma Well, located a few miles north of the castle but part of the same monument, is certainly one of the most unusual geological corners of the Southwest. Two hundred feet in diameter, this large limestone sink appears as a small spring-fed lake placed in a deep round cavity atop a hill. Through its outlet flow a half million gallons of water per day. Ducks swim on its usually calm surface, coots poke along reed-lined shores, and in recent years, late afternoon visitors could watch a Great Horned Owl on its nest in the surrounding cliff. In that semi-arid, dusty region, Montezuma Well is a true surprise; its long popularity in prehistoric times as a place to live is of little wonder.

The area surrounding the well was first permanently inhabited by Hohokam in the seventh century. Expert desert farmers, they dug approximately a mile of irrigation ditches from the well's outlet to an estimated sixty acres of garden plots. In the twelfth century, these Hohokam were joined by Sinagua from the northern plateau region. Between 1300 and 1400, the population of 150 to 200 people drew together for security, deserting most of their farming outposts. This consolidation, combined with defensive building, was probably in response to external threat and foreshadowed abandonment in the early 1400s.

At Montezuma Well, a short trail leads up from the parking lot to the rim of the hill overlooking the inner lake and ruins. Visitors need about fifteen minutes to reach this overlook. Here the trail divides into two branches, one winding down to the water's edge, passing by some small cliff ruins and the well's outlet, and the other bearing right at the rim to a larger pueblo complex. At least an hour should be planned to take both trails.

An interesting feature located along the road less than a mile from Montezuma Well is the roofed-over remains of a Hohokam pithouse. Many pithouses have been excavated over the years throughout the Southwest, but few have been preserved. Although only the floor remains to be seen, a cut-away scale model of the prepueblo dwelling is on exhibit to illustrate how it originally appeared.

Travel facilities can be found at Sedona, Cottonwood, and elsewhere, and several National Park Service campgrounds are available nearby. Tuzigoot National Monument, another major Sinagua ruin, is only twenty-seven miles to the east.

Suggested reading: *Montezuma Castle* by Albert H. Schroeder and Homer F. Hastings. National Park Service Historical Handbook Series No. 27. 1958. (Reprint 1961)

Tonto Basin from cave dwelling, Tonto National Monument

THE SALADO

Like the Sinagua, the Salado Indians developed a culture that blended Anasazi, Hohokam, and Mogollon traits. Originating along the Little Colorado in north-central Arizona, Salado culture expanded south to the headwaters of the Gila and Salt (*salado* is Spanish for "salt") Rivers. Although archaeologists do not agree on whether Salado culture came about through an actual movement of people or by a spread of ideas and practices, it is clear that the expansion was most active first in about A.D. 1100, then again in about 1300.

The Salado intermingled peacefully with resident Hohokam groups from whom they learned irrigation farming and the crafts of working stone and shell. Bringing with them knowledge of above-ground masonry building, they acted as a cultural conduit between the Anasazi to the north and the Mogollon to the southeast. Archaeologists recognize the principal Salado cultural trademark as a pottery style known as Gila Polychrome, which was made between the late thirteenth and early fifteenth centuries. Most other Salado traits on the archaeological record are indistinguishable from those of their Hohokam and Anasazi neighbors.

Salado culture remained intact until the early 1400s, when it either was absorbed by other groups or underwent such internal modification that its descendants are not identifiable as Salado. The last traces of Gila Polychrome pottery, dating to about 1450, have been found to the east and south, suggesting a possible absorp-

tion into Mogollon-derived communities in southern New Mexico.

Roosevelt Dam, constructed in 1911, flooded the Tonto Basin, forming Roosevelt Lake and inundating most of the archaeological remains of Salado culture. Since the science of archaeology in America was in its infancy at this time, many questions concerning this group of prehistoric people remain unanswered. Salado sites open to the public are the Upper and Lower Ruins at Tonto National Monument (see below) and the pueblo of Besh Ba Gowah in Globe (p. 116).

Tonto National Monument

Tonto National Monument is located on Arizona 88, 2 miles east of Roosevelt and 28 miles northwest of Globe. Driving time from Phoenix is about four hours.

From the Lower Ruin at Tonto National Monument, one's gaze can sweep down through the saguaro on the hillside below and over the vastness of the Tonto Basin. Except for the distant expanse of Roosevelt Lake, this is virtually the same view that the Salado occupants of these cliff dwellings had of their lands seven hundred years ago; neither the climate nor vegetation has changed appreciably.

Migrants from the north, the Salado built their homes close by their cultivated fields on the Salt River floodplain. They were close neighbors of the Hohokam, who were much earlier residents of the area and accomplished irrigation farmers. Among the crops raised were corn, pumpkins, squash, gourds, several varieties of beans, cotton, and grain amaranth. Acorns, agave, various types of cactus, cat-claw, acacia beans, cocklebur seeds, hackberry, juniper berries, mesquite beans, yucca, wild grapes, and walnuts are some of the wild food plants contributing to the Salado diet. Vorsila Bohrer, an ethnobotanist who analyzed the materials at Tonto, recorded that "the plant material...is perfectly preserved. Dried lima beans look like ones that might have come in a cellophane package on the grocery shelf."

In the mid-1200s, some of the Salado moved up to the impregnable cliff sites a thousand feet in altitude and several miles in distance above their croplands. Here, in cliff recesses, they constructed the dwellings of Tonto National Monument. This move, motivated by warfare, must have represented a great inconvenience for these farmers.

Dry cave sites, with their good preservation of perishable materials, are of great archaeological value, and the ruins of Tonto, despite sixty years of vandalism by settlers, are no exception. The Monument's three major sites, Upper Ruin, Lower Ruin, and Lower Ruin Annex, yielded not only the ethnobotanical remains mentioned above but also textiles of cotton, yucca, and hair, plaited yucca leaf sandals, basketry, matting, and cordage. A thirty-inch bow of netleaf hackberry, a tough shock-resistant wood, was recovered as well as such household items as fire-making equipment, fiber pot rests, brushes, torches, stirring sticks, tattoo needles, gums and adhesives, and spinning and weaving implements. Weapons found included bows, arrows, and clubs. Some ceremonial objects found were prayer sticks, charms, paint daubers, reed cigarettes, dice, and a ceremonial bow.

In considering the prehistoric life of the Tonto people, one can observe the cliff dwellings and countryside and try to fit the objects found by archaeologists into a logical and sensible picture. To scientists, this is a complex and difficult task; the casual visitor, however, is free to inject a liberal measure of imagination to bring the image into focus.

Visitors can hike up to the Lower Ruins along a half-mile trail from the visitor center. A trail guide offers much helpful information about the identity of plants along the walk. The round trip takes about forty-five minutes. The Upper Ruins may be visited with a ranger; persons interested in this longer excursion should call in advance for reservations.

Several cultural exhibits relating to the Tonto cliff dwellings are on display at the visitor center, and a picnic area is located near the parking lot. Food and lodging can be found at Roosevelt, and numerous camping spots are available in the vicinity of the monument.

An additional attraction to visiting Tonto is the scenic drive on Arizona 88 from Apache Junction to Roosevelt. This tortuous, partly unpaved road offers some of the best desert-mountain views in the Southwest. Travelers should be warned, however, that some sections of the road are closed to vehicles over thirty feet in length and that driving speed averages twenty to thirty miles per hour.

Suggested reading: *Archaeological Studies at Tonto National Monument, Arizona,* by Charlie R. Steen, Lloyd M. Pierson, Vorsila L. Bohrer, and Kate Peck Kent. Southwestern Monuments Association, 1962.

Right: Tonto's lower ruins

Besh Ba Gowah Ruins

Besh Ba Gowah Ruins are located 1.5 miles from the center of Globe, Arizona, 87 miles east of Phoenix on U.S. 60. To reach the site, follow South Broad Street to Ice House Canyon Road and continue to the Besh Ba Gowah sign on the right.

Besh Ba Gowah is an Apache word meaning "metal camp" and refers to the intensive mining operations around Globe, Arizona. Besh Ba Gowah Ruins, however, is a Salado pueblo consisting of 200 rooms and seven plazas dating from around A.D. 1225 to 1400. The pueblo sits on a mesa overlooking Pinal Creek, a tributary of the Salt River, and is surrounded by the eight thousand-foot Pinal Mountains to the southwest and the Apache Mountains to the north. The presence of numerous other ruins in the vicinity testifies to a large prehistoric population in the region.

Besh Ba Gowah's architecture was of rubble and adobe; river cobbles were carried up to the site and mortared into the walls with adobe from the mesa. The presence at the site of stored beans and corn as well as many stone hoes indicates that the village inhabitants were agriculturalists. Cotton apparently was used for clothing. The presence of pottery from distant areas, of copper bells presumably from Mexico, and ornaments made of shell from the Gulf of California, all suggest that Besh Ba Gowah was active in trade.

Salado culture is considered a blend of native or local traditions with influences from the Hohokam and Pueblo cultures. Salado sites are found quite extensively in the upper Salt and Gila regions. Irene Vickrey, who excavated Besh Ba Gowah in the late 1930s, suggested that factors such as drought or pestilence may have been responsible for the site's abandonment.

Besh Ba Gowah Ruins are administered by the city of Globe and are open at all times. Some artifacts from the site are on display at City Hall. Travel services are available in Globe and in nearby towns.

Pueblos and Missions of the Rio Grande

From the first, beginning in the late 1500s, the Spaniards identified their attempts to change the Indians of this region as a mission for civilizing a savage people. The missionaries, the military captains, and the colonial administrators were very conscious of this mission and of themselves as the bearers of civilization. The Spaniards identified civilization... by and large with the Castilian variety of the Spanish language, with adobe and stone houses, with men's trousers, with political organization focused through loyalty and obedience to the King of Spain, and with the Roman Catholic form of Christianity.

Edward H. Spicer

It is difficult to visualize what life was like for the Spanish explorers who penetrated the American Southwest over four centuries ago. It is even harder to imagine the impact these mounted, armored soldiers had on the indigenous peoples they encountered along their journey. Many Spanish records were lost in the Pueblo Revolt of 1680, and what little we know of events in the Rio Grande Valley over four hundred years ago has no doubt been distorted and romanticized over time.

And yet, to go to Pecos, Quarai, or Jemez and lay one's hand on the ponderous walls of mission churches built by Pueblo Indians and Spanish priests is to feel the past literally at one's fingertips. The intervening centuries may not melt away, but they are at least given an immediacy and substance that no history book or novel can duplicate.

The moment of contact between Pueblo Indian and European explorer came with Coronado's storming of the Zuni village of Hawikuh in 1540, roughly three centuries after the peak of Anasazi culture in the San Juan Basin. Pueblo culture had since regrouped into large communities in the Zuni Mountains, along the Little Colorado River, in the area of the Hopi mesas, and especially in the Rio Grande Valley between the present-day towns of Socorro and Taos. Coronado, with his party of three hundred soldiers and Christianized Mexican Indian servants, endured a long, fruitless quest that took a heavy toll in human life. It also established an adversary relationship between European and Indian that would last long after the collapse of the Spanish Empire.

After Coronado, fifty-seven years elapsed before another colonizing expedition to these northern lands was organized by Juan de Oñate, who traveled with four hundred followers including Franciscan missionaries. This time, the Spaniards intended to stay. Oñate obtained pledges of allegiance and obedience from Pueblo *caciques* and laid claim to 87,000 square miles of territory in the name of the king. His religious counterparts, meanwhile, claimed thousands of souls for Christ. What these pledges and conversions actually meant to the Indians involved was not recorded and probably not known by Spanish chroniclers.

The early conquistadores encoun-

Tyuonyi ruins, Bandelier National Monument

tered over sixty Pueblo villages whose inhabitants spoke many dialects of at least four distinct Pueblo languages. Most significantly, from a military standpoint, these North American natives were living in small, autonomous communities that had no social or political unity with their neighbors. The several hundred Spaniards, therefore, were not pitted against tens of thousands of Indians. Rather, the invaders faced a series of challenges posed by separate villages or groups of villages, none of which had a population much over two thousand and most less than five hundred.

The typical Rio Grande pueblo of this period was a compact community with large adobe apartment houses built around a central court. Houses normally were entered by means of rooftop hatchways; interior groups of rooms were interconnected by small doorways. Except in bad weather, most living activities and household chores took place on the roofs and in the plazas. These Indians were accomplished agriculturalists whose staples consisted of corn plus various types of beans, squash, and pumpkins.

They frequently raised turkeys in pens bordering the plazas and carried on a long tradition of hunting game and gathering edible plants, seeds, nuts, and fruit. Rio Grande culture, which had developed from an essentially Mogollon base, had received a substantial impetus in the thirteenth century with the arrival of many dislocated Anasazi from the Four Corners region. These migrants, many from Mesa Verde, successfully adapted to the new region with its many natural resources. By the mid-sixteenth century, Rio Grande Pueblo population had increased to an estimated thirty to forty thousand.

When Coronado visited the Rio Grande pueblos in 1540–41, he heard stories of attacks by Plains Apaches or Caddoans that had taken place twenty-five years earlier at some eastern villages. In fact, the Spanish movement into the Rio Grande Valley from the south roughly coincided with intrusion from the north and east by nomadic Apaches. The Pueblo people—well-established, productive farmers that they were—found themselves caught in a squeeze between two demand-

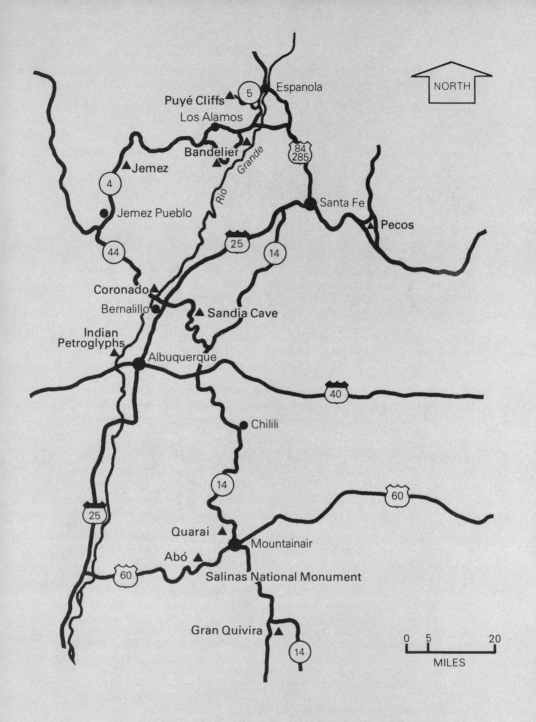

NORTH

Espanola

Puyé Cliffs ▲

⑤

Los Alamos ●

Bandelier ▲

Rio Grande

Jemez ▲

④

Jemez Pueblo ●

㉘㉘ 84 285

Santa Fe ●

Pecos ▲

㉕

⑭

44

Coronado ▲

Bernalillo ●

▲ Sandia Cave

Indian Petroglyphs ▲

Albuquerque ●

㊵ 40

Chilili ●

㉕ 25

⑭

⑥ 60

Quarai ▲

Abó ▲

Mountainair ●

Salinas National Monument

60 ⑥

Gran Quivira ▲

⑭

0   5   20

MILES

Rio Grande Area

ing, often hostile invasions. Out of this situation, complex relationships developed. The Plains tribes, including the Comanches by the 1700s, periodically plundered the pueblos. They also exchanged meat and skins for Pueblo corn or sold slaves in return for Spanish guns. The Spaniards developed a legalized system of tribute known as the *encomienda,* a right proffered to a Spaniard to collect tribute from a given community of Pueblo Indians. Tribute included such items as shawls, corn, buckskins, piñon nuts, and labor. Slavery, particularly of orphans, was also practiced. Under this system, the Spanish colony grew in size and strength; priests ventured into the hinterlands to build missions such as Abó, Quarai, Gran Quivira, Pecos, and Jemez, and in some cases, surpluses were accumulated for export to Mexico City. Oñate introduced forty priests to the new territory in 1598. These Franciscans were dedicated, courageous, enterprising men, persistent in the face of adversity. Their churches, although constructed from a pool of Indian labor, are testimony of their organizational and architectural capabilities.

Through contact with Spanish soldiers, settlers, and priests, the Pueblo Indian was introduced to new crops, sheep and cattle husbandry, new technology, and Western education. Additionally, the *encomenderos* were responsible for protecting their villages from external attack. But on balance, the Spanish occupation was a heavy burden to the Indians of New Mexico. Theirs had always been a marginal existence, and in many cases, the economic deprivations suffered under Spanish rule brought hunger, disease, and social disruption. By the late 1600s, especially during the drought of 1667 to 1672, all groups were experiencing hardships, and relationships deteriorated. At this time, the pueblos of Las Salinas Province, to the southeast of Albuquerque, received the

worst impact of both drought and depredation by Apaches and Comanches. Abó, Quarai, and Gran Quivira were abandoned. During the same period, the Spanish colony experienced growing incompatibility between civil and ecclesiastical authorities who disputed over the distribution of goods and labor extracted from the Indians. With the Franciscans unable to fill their missionary quota, civil authorities growing corrupt, Plains tribes on the attack, and a crop-withering drought in the offing, the situation in New Mexico in the 1660s and 1670s was at a low ebb.

In 1680, under the leadership of Popé, a San Juan Indian, the pueblos united briefly in a well-planned revolt that resulted in the killing of nearly four hundred Spanish colonists and priests and the eviction of the remaining two thousand members of the colony. The defeated Spanish regrouped around El Paso and were joined by a few southern Pueblo villages who had not participated in the revolt. Here they remained for twelve years before returning and reconquering under Don Diego de Vargas. Following this brief period of Pueblo supremacy, the northern Rio Grande region underwent gradual settlement by Spanish, then Mexican, and finally Anglo-American peoples. Contrary to all the efforts and expectations of the successive conquering groups, however, Pueblo society remained remarkably intact and has continued to the present day.

The archaeological monuments of Abó, Quarai, Gran Quivira, Pecos, and Jemez all date to the seventeenth century, a fascinating period of New Mexican history marked by the tumultuous coming together of three different peoples with largely incompatible cultural traditions. Today, a visitor to a northern Rio Grande pueblo can stand in front of a Roman Catholic

Right: San Gregorio de Abó mission

church across from a kiva, and watch Indians with Spanish surnames doing a "Comanche Dance." Afterwards, a dancer might very possibly drive off in an American car to a job in the atomic city of Los Alamos.

Suggested reading: *Cycles of Conquest,* by Edward Spicer. University of Arizona Press, 1962.

Bandelier National Monument

Bandelier National Monument is located 46 miles west of Santa Fe, New Mexico. From Santa Fe, follow U.S. 285 north to Pojoaque, then bear left on State 4 and continue 24 miles to the monument's entrance.

About 4 P.M. the border of the almost precipitous descent into the Cañon de los Frijoles was reached, and it took one-half hour to descend— on foot, of course. The grandest thing I ever saw. A magnificent growth of pines, encina, alamos, and towering cliffs, of pumice or volcanic tuff, exceedingly friable. The cliffs are vertical on the north side, and their bases are, for a length as yet unknown to me, used as dwellings both from the inside, and by inserting the roof poles for stories outside. It is of the highest interest. There are some of one, two, and three stories. In most cases the plaster is still in the rooms. Some are walled in; others are mere holes in the rocks. Much pottery of the older, painted sort, but as yet no corrugated ones. I found entire chimneys, metates, manos and a stone-axe.

Adolph F. Bandelier, 1880

One of the motifs of this guidebook is the early appearance of Adolph F.

Bandelier at outstanding ruins throughout the Southwest. Frijoles Canyon, in the middle of the Pajarito Plateau, just west of the Rio Grande in northern New Mexico, was visited by Bandelier and his Cochiti Indian guides on October 23, 1880. It is altogether fitting that the national monument established in this rich archaeological and natural environment should bear his name.

In 1880, Bandelier arrived in Santa Fe to begin an extraordinary career of anthropological exploration and discovery that would make his name legend among archaeologists, ethnographers, and historians for generations to come. His mission was to acquire as much knowledge as possible about the culture and history of Indians living in the Southwest, a land whose native peoples were little understood by the many new settlers arriving from St. Louis and points east. Surviving on a small allowance, Bandelier covered great distances on foot, befriended natives, and encountered formidable obstacles of weather, terrain, fatigue, and sickness. His pioneering efforts as an observer of customs, recorder of story and myth, and surveyor of prehistoric ruins established him as the first anthropological scholar of the Southwest.

One of the first archaeologists to follow Bandelier was Edgar Lee Hewett. Hewett explored the plateau region where the monument is located more thoroughly than his predecessor and conducted numerous excavations, including those at Tyuonyi Ruins situated a short distance up Frijoles Canyon from the visitor center. As an archaeologist, Hewett was deeply impressed by the entire Pajarito Plateau and lobbied for the establishment of an extensive "National Park of the Cliff Cities." Although his aspirations were on a larger scale than could be realized, he was successful in 1916 in having forty-two square miles of the plateau set aside, principally to con-

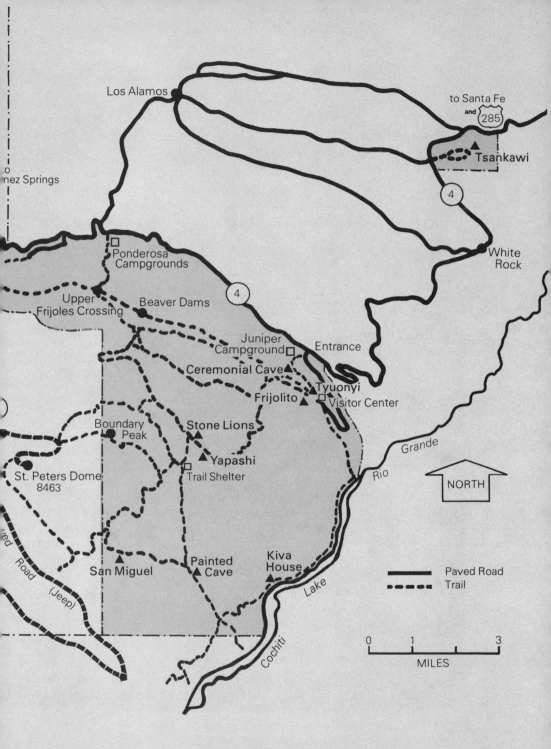

to Santa Fe
and 285

Los Alamos

Tsankawi

4

Jemez Springs

White
Rock

Ponderosa
Campgrounds

Upper
Frijoles Crossing

Beaver Dams

4

Juniper
Campground

Entrance

Ceremonial Cave

Frijolito

Tyuonyi
Visitor Center

Stone Lions

Boundary
Peak

Yapashi
Trail Shelter

Grande

St. Peters Dome
8463

Rio

NORTH

San Miguel

Painted
Cave

Kiva
House

Lake

Road (Jeep)

Cochiti

Paved Road
Trail

0   1   3

MILES

Bandelier National Monument

Adolph F. Bandelier, 1840–1914. Courtesy of the Museum of New Mexico.

serve its archaeological heritage. Much of the remaining Pajaritan area that concerned Hewett is under the strict control and protection of the Los Alamos Scientific Laboratory and has been off-limits to the public since the early years of World War II.

The Pajarito Plateau is a long shelf of compressed volcanic ash and basaltic lava reaching from the vicinity of Cochiti Pueblo at its southern end to near Santa Clara Pueblo at the north. It was formed just over a million years ago as a consequence of volcanic eruptions to the west of the monument. Over time, as the soft porous tuff submitted to the forces of erosion, many deep canyons separated by long narrow mesas were formed. This sequence of uplands and valleys provided a varied and hospitable environment for the region's Indian inhabitants of relatively recent times. It also formed a landscape that delights today's hikers and sightseers as much as it did earlier explorers and pioneers.

The monument area was first used by nomadic big game hunters thousands of years before the beginning of the Christian era. Little is known of the activities of these early North American people, either in New Mexico or elsewhere, but the discovery of several Folsom points (early man spearheads) on the plateau strongly suggests that these people came here, at least occasionally, to hunt. They were followed by seminomadic hunters and gatherers, whose campsites have been found by archaeologists especially around sand dunes along the Rio Grande. These Archaic people, ancestors of the Pueblo Indians, moved about in family groups to take advantage of game patterns and seasonal availability of naturally occurring plant resources.

During the early Rio Grande Pueblo period (A.D. 600 to 1200), there is little evidence that the area of Bandelier National Monument had any permanent population. From this point on, however, population increased and was affected by the movement of Anasazi from the Four Corners region to the Rio Grande Valley. The ruins of Tyuonyi, the many cliff and cave dwellings, and numerous other pueblos at the monument date from approximately A.D. 1200 to 1500.

These Pajaritan settlers first built and occupied small, scattered, one-family or extended family pueblos on the mesas near areas in which they raised corn, beans, and squash. Many of these small sites have been located, and archaeologists believe that they were occupied for short periods of time, a generation or less, as these small agricultural groups exploited an area and moved on. Later, as population increased and the Pajaritan people further adapted to their environment, they established villages of considerably larger size, often in the canyons and at the base of canyon cliffs. Many pueblos number 100 to 200 rooms; a few with over 500 and even 1000 or more rooms have been recorded. Frequently these pueblos were built around a central plaza with room-blocks stepped back to a height of several stories. The cliff and cave dwellings were strung along the tops of talus slopes on the north side of canyons. Natural caves or hollows in the soft tuff were enlarged into rooms or kivas and often were fronted by multistoried masonry structures. Many dwellings like this can be visited in Frijoles Canyon, close to the monument's visitor center.

Prehistoric life in the canyon centered around farming plots of corn, beans, and squash along the bottomlands, often utilizing check dams and small-scale irrigation techniques. Water, both as precipitation and as run-off in Frijoles Creek, was plentiful. The Jemez Mountains were rich in game, and the natural environment offered a wealth of edible plants. Under such conditions, Pajaritan culture flourished here for over three centuries. In the early sixteenth cen-

Frijoles cave dwelling, Bandelier National Monument

Left: Long House ruins, Bandelier National Monument

tury, however, conditions did change, and the population of Frijoles Canyon and surrounding areas moved down to settlements closer to the Rio Grande. This abandonment of the plateau preceded Spanish colonization of the northern Rio Grande region by only half a century. The descendents of the Pajaritan people presently live in the pueblos of San Ildefonso, Santa Clara, and Cochiti.

Bandelier National Monument offers a variety of activities for visitors, from picnicking in the shade of cottonwoods next to one's car to backpacking trips using the sixty-five miles of maintained trails. Whatever one chooses to do, archaeological sites in the form of pueblo ruins, cave dwellings, rock art, or religious shrines will not be far distant. Maps and guidebooks are available at the monument headquarters. Most visitors to Bandelier see only the Frijoles Canyon sites, for which a detailed trail guide is available. One can spend anywhere from an hour to half a day in the canyon seeing Tyuonyi, the caves (some can be entered by ladder), Long House, and Ceremonial Cave. Many faint petroglyphs can be seen above some of the ruins. In the caves, one can get out of the sun, enjoy a beautiful view of the canyon and tree-lined creek, and let one's imagination run back five centuries to a time when the area was alive with the activities of hundreds of Indians.

Other more distant archaeological sites include the Frijolito Ruin (one mile roundtrip), Stone Lions Shrine (twelve miles roundtrip), Painted Cave (twenty miles roundtrip), and the pueblo sites of San Miguel, Yapashi, and Kiva House, all requiring long hikes. Also of interest are the ruins of Tsankawi, located in a separate section of the monument eleven miles north on State 4. This archaeological area is passed on the left hand side of the road when driving to the main monument from Santa Fe. Tsankawi is

an unexcavated pueblo, and caves similar to those of Frijoles Canyon are found behind it. The trail loop in the Tsankawi section is one and a half miles long, very scenic, and passes a fascinating spot where footwear over the centuries has worn a deep narrow trench in the soft rock. Many people on their way to Frijoles pass by the Tsankawi turnoff without stopping, and for this reason it is often a quieter and more private place to visit.

Facilities at the monument include a campground, picnic area, interpretive museum and audio-visual program, and snack bar with camping supplies. More overnight lodging as well as gas stations and other travel services can be found in Los Alamos, Espanola, or along U.S. 285.

Suggested reading: *Bandelier National Monument: Geology, History, Prehistory.* School of American Research, Santa Fe, 1980.

Puyé Cliff Dwellings

Puyé Cliff Dwellings are located on the Santa Clara Indian Reservation 11 miles west of Espanola, New Mexico, on State Route 5. Driving distances from Los Alamos and Santa Fe are approximately 25 and 40 miles, respectively.

Puyé (poo-yay) Mesa, the location of a large pueblo site and extensive cliff dwellings, affords an unparalleled view over the broad northern Rio Grande Valley. To the west lie the Jemez Mountains, the product of violent volcanic activity a million years ago, and across the Rio Grande to the east rise the Sangre de Cristos, the southernmost spur of the Rocky Mountains. One has to remind oneself

Puyé ruins

that in choosing this home site, the prehistoric inhabitants of the mesa had more basic requirements in mind than scenery.

Like Tyuonyi Ruins at nearby Bandelier National Monument, Puyé Pueblo was constructed of blocks of tuff, a lightweight, porous, volcanic rock that is easily shaped with stone tools. This soft but durable material, which is found so abundantly on the Pajarito Plateau, was an important natural resource contributing to the intense architectural activity here in the thirteenth through fifteenth centuries. Puyé, with over one thousand rooms, is one of the two largest pueblos in the region. Its multistoried roomblocks, terraced back in a manner similar to Taos Pueblo, form a large quadrangle around an inner court.

Running for over a mile along the cliff below the pueblo are two levels of cave dwellings; most were formerly fronted by masonry rooms of several stories. Some of the latter have been reconstructed to give a better idea of how the community appeared in prehistoric times. All the caves along the mesa can be explored at will, making this an area especially exciting (and potentially hazardous) for children. At the foot of the mesa, a creek flowing out of Santa Clara Canyon provides not only drinking water but also water for irrigating cultivated fields in the bottomland.

Puyé Pueblo was the first Rio Grande pueblo to be systematically excavated, but unfortunately, only general descriptive notes were kept and no detailed report ever published. In the early years of southwestern archaeological research, it was common to place more emphasis on opening up ruins and recovering artifacts than on scientific reportage.

The Santa Clara Indians, who own and maintain this site and whose pueblo lies seven miles east of the

Puyé cliff dwellings

mesa, regard the Puyé people as their direct ancestors. Each summer, the Santa Clarans hold a weekend ceremonial at the site that includes dances and a fair. The public is welcome.

A road winds up the mesa to the pueblo, where one can park and walk through the partially restored ruins. Trails to the cliff dwellings can be taken from either the bottom or top of the mesa. The only disappointing aspect of a visit to Puyé is the absence of archaeological or cultural interpretation at the site. Persons considering a visit here should also note that the monument is closed in winter and that even during its open season, the entrance gate is occasionally locked. One might wish to call the Santa Clara tribal offices in advance to make sure the ruins will be open on a given date. The monument has fresh water, toilets, and a picnic site; nearby Santa Clara Canyon has a campground and fishing stream. Travel services can be found in Espanola, Los Alamos, or Santa Fe.

Suggested reading: *Pajarito Plateau Archaeological Survey and Excavations,* by Charlie R. Steen. The Los Alamos Scientific Laboratory of the University of California, 1977.

Indian Petroglyphs State Park

Indian Petroglyphs State Park is located off Atrisco Drive, northwest of downtown Albuquerque, New Mexico. From Interstate 40, drive north on Coors Boulevard to Montano Road. Turn left on Montano, proceed 2 miles to Atrisco, turn right, and continue 0.5 miles to the park's entrance gate.

The geology and climate of the American Southwest lend themselves to the creation of rock art. In many cases, a drawing etched into the desert varnish of an exposed boulder or cliff face will remain virtually unchanged for generation after generation of passing viewers. Rock art sites are found in areas that were at one time frequented by people — along trade routes and game trails, near habitations and springs, and at sacred places. Sometimes it is difficult to determine why a given spot was chosen.

The rock art site at Indian Petroglyphs State Park is believed to have been associated with an early Pueblo hunting area or to have had special spiritual significance. Here, and at other sites in the vicinity, hundreds of petroglyphs were drawn on volcanic boulders at the edge of an ancient lava flow. Against the darkened surface of these half-million- to a million-year-old rocks, the artwork stands out as white or grey lines.

The hill on which these petroglyphs appear looks out over the wide expanse of the Rio Grande Valley, whose fertile soils sustained many prehistoric Pueblo communities. Behind the river, the ten thousand-foot crests of the Sandia Mountains rise over the haze of Albuquerque like the painted backdrop of a movie set. In years past, the mountains provided game, food resources, and building materials to the Indians. The petroglyphs were made by these Anasazi descendents beginning around A.D. 1100 and continuing until the time of Spanish contact five hundred years later. In the early 1600s, Pueblo culture changed drastically, many villages were abandoned, and native populations declined.

These petroglyphs are not the clean, crisp, highly readable type often seen on the sandstone cliffs and rock ledges of the Colorado Plateau and in Utah. Many are rough or thinly scratched, others faint from weathering. Trails wind up the volcanic talus slope among the boulders on which are pecked or rubbed the images of humans, animals, birds, and plants, as well as ceremonial

designs and masks. Here and there are rock shelters, grinding spots where stone tools were fashioned, and other evidence of human presence. There is little literature on the rock art of this site, little to learn about the history or significance of the site or the individual petroglyphs beyond what the viewer can discover through his own powers of observation, common sense, reflection, and intuition. But the pictures themselves hold much fascination and tell a story of their own about the life of their creators. In addition, viewers will certainly feel excitement at finding written signs left by a long ago people whom we will never meet.

Along the park's driving loop there are numerous turnoffs from which visitors can walk the hilly petroglyph trails. The park is open from 10:00 A.M. to 6:00 P.M. April through October and from 9:00 A.M. to 5:00 P.M. the rest of the year. It is closed on Tuesday and Wednesday. A picnic area and toilets are available. One should plan on at least an hour to see the entire site.

Suggested reading: *Rock Art in New Mexico,* by Polly Schaafsma. New Mexico State Planning Office, Santa Fe, 1972.

Coronado State Monument

Coronado State Monument is located on the west bank of the Rio Grande 1 mile northwest of Bernalillo, New Mexico, on State 44.

Situated on an exposed, arid rise of land, the ruins of Kuaua Pueblo overlook the perpetual life force of the Rio Grande. Across the river to the east

Left: Petroglyphs of human figures, Indian Petroglyphs State Park

rise the nearly eleven thousand-foot peaks of the Sandia Mountains, while in all other directions rolling grasslands abound. The pueblo's waist-high mud walls, eroding under each passing storm, are a reminder of a life and culture that flourished here for more than three hundred years.

Kuaua is a superb archaeological example of the Rio Grande pueblo. Constructed around A.D. 1300 of coursed adobe, it consisted of large multistoried roomblocks surrounding three spacious plazas with underground kivas. Like many prehistoric pueblos, Kuaua was a veritable fortress, its high, exterior, doorless walls serving as bulwarks from which to fend off potential attack. Entrance was gained only by narrow passageways.

The inhabitants of Kuaua were Tiwa-speaking Indians, descendents of the Anasazi, and ancestors of the present-day residents of Sandia and Isleta pueblos. The Kuauans were farmers who raised corn, beans, and squash in irrigated fields on the alluvial plain along the Rio Grande. They also went on hunting and gathering forays in the mountains across the river, where archaeologists have found their characteristic glazeware pottery around the entrance to Sandia Cave. Apart from defending themselves against periodic Apache raids, the Kuauans probably led a very peaceful existence until the arrival of the Spanish in the sixteenth century. A first-hand account of Tiwa life at the time of contact can be found in the chronicles of Pedro de Casteñeda de Naxera, who accompanied the Coronado expedition.

Life at Kuaua lasted only briefly into the European era of New Mexican history. It was the northernmost of twelve Tiwa villages in what Spanish chroniclers called the Province of Tigueax along the middle Rio Grande. Coronado State Monument, which encompasses the Kuaua ruins, is named in recognition of the 1540–41

Kuaua ruins, Coronado State Monument

Kuaua kiva mural, Coronado State Monument

expedition led by the famed conquistador Francisco Vásquez de Coronado. Coronado and his followers, disappointed by the lack of gold at the Zuni pueblos to the west, exhausted by their arduous journey, plagued by a frigid winter, and hungry, arrived in the area of Kuaua in an ungenerous mood. What hospitality and compassion the Pueblo population offered them on arrival dissipated when the Spaniards began to appropriate food and clothing. The relationship soon deteriorated into open hostility, siege, the massacre of Pueblo people and temporary abandonment by the Indians of all the villages in the vicinity. This experience marked the beginning of a long, trying relationship between Native American and European that was to continue four hundred years and longer. Kuaua was permanently abandoned around 1700 when increased Spanish settlement and influence caused the scattered Tiwa pueblos to consolidate. Of the dozen Tiwa communities recorded by the Spanish in the sixteenth century, only two remain today.

During the 1930s, 1200 rooms at this site were excavated by the Museum of New Mexico, University of New Mexico, and School of American Research. The restoration of much of the pueblo at this time to first floor level accounts for the adobe brick construction visible in the walls today. The great archaeological and artistic find at Kuaua was the now famous square kiva with its seventeen layers of multicolored frescos. This discovery represents the first extensive prehistoric mural art found in New Mexico and one of the most outstanding examples in North America. The kiva, which has been reconstructed with full-scale reproductions of the frescos, may be entered by means of a smoke hole ladder and is certainly the high point of a visit to this site. Visitors who have been to Aztec Ruins will be particularly interested in comparing this unique ceremonial chamber to Aztec's great kiva. Together they represent two very different expressions of

Anasazi religious architecture and art.

Coronado State Monument's small museum includes excellent cultural exhibits that are interesting to see prior to taking the self-guiding interpretive trail through the ruins. The monument is closed Tuesdays, Wednesdays, and holidays. Coronado State Park, next to the monument, offers picnic sites and camping. Sandia Cave (see p. 150), near Placitas, and Indian Petroglyphs (p. 131), on the northwestern outskirts of Albuquerque, are two other nearby archaeological sites.

Pecos National Monument

Pecos National Monument is located off I-25, approximately 25 miles southeast of Santa Fe, New Mexico. From Santa Fe, take the Glorieta-Pecos exit and proceed 8 miles to the Monument. Travelers coming from the east on I-25 should take the Rowe exit and continue 3 miles to the ruins.

In 1927, Alfred V. Kidder invited his colleagues to join him at Pecos Ruins to discuss common archaeological problems and concerns. Kidder was nearing the completion of ten years of excavations at Pecos, an enterprise that would become a landmark in the history of New World archaeology. In addition to participating in wide-ranging discussions on the status of southwestern archaeology, Kidder's peers had an opportunity to witness the results of his painstakingly detailed and systematic excavation methods. His work at this site represented a shift from a traditional emphasis on artifact collecting for museums to a focus on the science of recovering and interpreting archaeological data. Kidder's accomplishments at Pecos, which were later

The church at Pecos

published in multiple volumes, were unprecedented for their thoroughness and greatly influenced his own and later generations of American archaeologists.

Pecos Pueblo is situated on a rocky knoll in the middle of a large fertile valley in north-central New Mexico. The nearby Pecos River flows out of high mountains to the north and continues nearly six hundred miles to empty into the Rio Grande in Texas. High mesas border the valley on its south side, and to the west the land rises to Glorieta Pass, with the broad valley of the Rio Grande lying beyond. To the east, the valley descends gradually and opens out on the southwestern sector of the Great Plains.

All this geography, beyond providing the Pecos people with a beautiful and varied environment in which to live, played a key role in the life and history of the pueblo. Close by were good farmlands and reliable springs. The surrounding high country provided

game-rich hunting territories, many varieties of plant food resources, and wood for building and fuel. Materials for making stone tools and weapons, pottery, and baskets were also close at hand. But what gave Pecos a special advantage was its strategic situation between the agricultural Pueblo communities of the northern Rio Grande and the nomadic hunting tribes of the Great Plains. Trade became a central factor in the pueblo's economy. This role, while no doubt profitable, was also precarious, and the Pecos people, who suffered repeatedly from Caddo, Apache, and Comanche depredations paid a heavy price for the benefits accrued by their favorable situation.

Pecos's history began between A.D. 800 and 1100, when growing populations along the Rio Grande expanded into the upper Pecos valley to form small, scattered settlements. As these farming groups consolidated, Pecos Pueblo was founded around

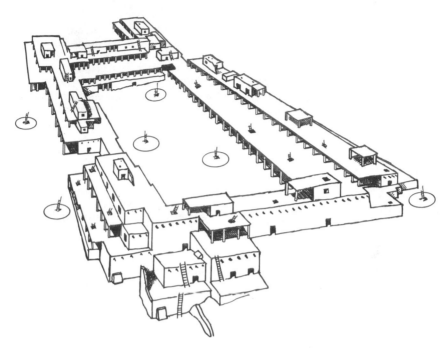

Reconstruction of North Pueblo, Pecos National Monument

A.D. 1300. Later, the pueblo grew to nearly seven hundred rooms arranged in a quadrangle of multistoried community houses around a large central plaza. The pueblo was constructed like a fortress with high outside walls without doors. From its ramparts, a clear view could be gained in all directions. A perimeter wall provided an initial defensive line against attackers. Pecos thrived until the early 1700s and actually continued to exist until 1838 when its seventeen final occupants journeyed eighty miles northwest to join relatives at Jemez.

Pecos was one of the first North American villages to feel the impact of European contact. Less than fifty years after Columbus first set foot in the Americas, this pueblo was visited by Coronado and his followers; the introduction was unproductive to both parties. Coronado, the first Spanish explorer to penetrate the American Southwest, had been disappointed thus far in his explorations. He and his exhausted men had endured the hardships of a northern New Mexico winter and inspired hatred for their depredations among Indian villages along the Rio Grande north of Albuquerque. Arriving at Pecos desperate to justify his expensive expedition from Mexico City, he was lured by the locals to pursue a fruitless treasure hunt east onto the plains. The Pecos *caciques* even provided a Plains Indian "guide" whom the Spaniards referred to as "the Turk."

After Coronado's visit, Pecos was spared further contact with the Spanish explorers until 1591, when Castaño de Sosa successfully attacked and occupied the pueblo with a force of thirty-seven men plus horses and cannons. In his account of the expedition, Castaño described the pueblo and its inhabitants as follows:

The houses in this pueblo are in the manner of houseblocks. They have doors to the outside all around, and the

137

houses are back to back. The houses are four and five stories. In the galleries [covered porches] there are no doors to the streets [on the ground-floor level]. They go up little ladders that can be pulled up by hand through the hatchways. Every house has 3 or 4 apartments [on each story] so that from top to bottom each house has 15 or 16 rooms. The rooms are worthy of note, being well whitewashed....

The dress of the men, according to what we saw there — as it was the cold season — most or all of them wore a blanket of cotton and a buffalo hide over it.... The women [dress] with a blanket drawn in a knot at the shoulder and a sash the width of a palm at the waist. At one side, the blanket is completely open. Over it are placed some other very gaily worked blanket or some turkey feather robes and many other curious things....

In 1620, Spanish monks of the Franciscan Order established a mission at Pecos that included a church and convent complete with carpenter shop, weaving rooms, tanneries, school, and living quarters. The Franciscans introduced wheat, bread making, European farming methods and tools, adobe building bricks, and cattle, goat, and sheep husbandry. The native economy and way of life was never the same again.

The Pecos mission was destroyed in the Pueblo Revolt of 1680 but rebuilt following the reconquest of 1692. Two significant dates stand out in the course of Pecos's eventual disintegration: 1750, when the pueblo's military force was massacred by Comanches; and 1788, when its population was struck by a smallpox epidemic. Pecos was caught, it seemed, between destructive forces totally beyond its control.

Pecos National Monument's most impressive ruins are the standing remains of the eighteenth-century church, with its massive adobe walls and arched doorways. The footings of an older and even larger church are also visible. Visitors should pick up a pamphlet to orient them around the site or join one of the guided tours that are conducted by National Park rangers. The ruins trail leads through the churches and adjoining convent, past excavated portions of the South Pueblo, and on to the large hilltop mounds of the North Pueblo. Along the route one can enter a reconstructed kiva. About half an hour is needed to see the church ruins, which are next to the monument's parking lot, and the time should be approximately doubled to tour the North Pueblo. On summer weekends, a "living history" program emphasizing traditional bread- and pottery-making demonstrations by local Hispanic and Indian craftspeople, is held at the visitor center.

Pecos Village, located about two miles from the monument, has several restaurants, grocery stores, and gas stations. A paved road leads north of the village up the Pecos River canyon to camp and picnic areas and good fishing spots. From Santa Fe, a trip to Pecos and the ruins makes a very pleasant half-day excursion.

Suggested reading: *Alfred V. Kidder,* by Richard B. Woodbury. Columbia University Press, 1973.
The Four Churches of Pecos, by Alden C. Hayes. University of New Mexico Press, 1974.
Pecos Ruins, School of American Research, Santa Fe, 1981.

Right: The church at Pecos

Jemez State Monument

Jemez State Monument is located on State 4 just north of Jemez Springs, New Mexico, 55 miles north of Albuquerque and 30 miles southwest of Los Alamos.

Each couple has its own place designated in accordance with the census list. When there are many, the married couples make two rows on each side, the two men in the middle and the women at the sides. This may seem a superficial matter, but it is not, for experience has taught me that when these women are together they spend all the time dedicated to prayer and Mass in gossip, showing one another their glass beads, ribbons and medals, etc., telling who gave them to them or how they obtained them and other mischief. Therefore, the religious who has charge of the administration must have care in this regard. After all, it is a house of prayer, not of chit-chat.

Father Joaquin de Jesús de Ruíz
Jemez, 1776

The Jemez (Háy-mez) Indians, like those of Zuni, Kuaua, and Pecos, were among the first native North Americans to encounter European explorers when, in 1541, Francisco de Barrio-Nuevo, one of Coronado's captains, penetrated into the southern Jemez Mountain region of north-central New Mexico. Counting seven Pueblo villages in the vicinity of Jemez Springs, the conquistador named this the province of *Aguas Calientes*. Fifty-seven years later, the Spanish colonizer Juan de Oñate counted eight Jemez villages and heard reports of three more.

Franciscan missionizing efforts among the Jemez in the early 1600s faltered at first. To simplify their task and to facilitate administrative control over the indigenous population, the Spaniards consolidated the scattered Jemez communities into three villages — Giusewa, Patoqua, and Astialakwa. But in 1622, Navajo raids resulted in the abandonment of Giusewa and Patoqua and the dispersal of their inhabitants. The new church at Giusewa also was destroyed. The Franciscan effort persisted, however, and by 1627, under the leadership of Fray Martín de Avenida, the Jemez people were reassembled and the church, San José de los Jemez, rebuilt.

The history of this mission was marked by conflict and misfortune. In the mid-1600s, the Jemez made peace with the Navajo and conspired unsuccessfully to evict the Spaniards. In 1680, they joined the Pueblo Revolt that succeeded in driving out or killing all Spanish priests, soldiers, civil servants, and settlers. Giusewa's resident Franciscan, Fray Juan de Jesús Maria, was martyrized at the church altar. Twelve years later, Vargas reconquered New Mexico and found the Jemez people living in one mesa-top pueblo. In 1693, the Jemez made war on Santa Ana and Zia pueblos, provoking a punitive strike by Vargas that drove them from their village and resulted in the deaths of 84 people with 361 taken prisoner. At this time, Vargas also recovered the body of Fray Maria in which he found an arrow still embedded in the shoulder. The indefatigable Jemez joined the abortive revolt of 1696 and afterwards fled west from their homeland to Navajo country. Several years later, they returned to found Walatoa, or Jemez Pueblo, where they have remained to the present day.

In 1921 and 1922, archaeologists from the School of American Research in Santa Fe excavated a section of Giusewa and found that the pueblo predated the church by at least three hundred years. The site has never been thoroughly surveyed, but its mounds are easily recognizable beginning on the west side of the church and extending across the present highway. It is thought that some por-

San José de los Jemez church, Jemez State Monument

tions of the pueblo once attained a height of three stories. Although twenty rooms and two kivas were cleared during these initial excavations, little scientific information was recorded for posterity.

The church and monastery, constructed of sandstone and adobe with walls varying in thickness from two to eight feet, was considerably more intact than the pueblo. Even in ruins, it is a truly impressive structure, the more so when one reflects on the fact that no secular architects or engineers were available to assist these early Franciscan priests and their Indian laborers. The interior of the church measures 111 feet in length and is 34 feet wide. Along the sides of the nave stand twelve pedestals that probably supported statues of the disciples.

Perhaps the most exciting discovery in the church ruins was a series of frescoes on the nave walls. The fresco technique, involving the application of paint to wet plaster, was rare in New Mexico ecclesiastical art. Fleur-de-lis and other floral patterns and realistic Indian motifs in green, blue, yellow, red, black, and white were found. Today, they are reproduced in the museum. Also of interest was the discovery of windows of selenite, a translucent form of gypsum. At the rear of the church, an octagonal turret rises forty-two feet above the altar, emphasizing the fact that seventeenth-century New Mexico churches served a defensive as well as religious function. In 1936 and 1937, the adjoining monastery was excavated, including numerous compartments used by the Franciscans, a small private chapel, and the remains of a stairway.

Jemez State Monument is administered by the Museum of New Mexico and is open from 9:00 A.M. to 5:00 P.M. except on Tuesdays, Wednesdays, and state holidays, when it is closed. Its small museum has interpretive exhibits relating to New Mexico history and displays of Indian and Spanish artifacts and crafts. The ruins trail passes over the mounds of Giusewa, past an open kiva, through the remains of the church and monastery, and into the courtyard. Signs along the path interpret features of historical interest. The monument is nestled at the edge of a narrow valley in piñon- and juniper-covered foothills. This beautiful landscape may attract some visitors to walk or explore further on their own.

Route 4 to Los Alamos offers an exceptionally scenic drive through the Jemez Mountains, past the Valle Grande to Bandelier National Monument (see p. 122). Camping areas and picnic grounds are available along the road. A few miles south of the monument is Jemez Pueblo, whose people are the descendents of the occupants of Giusewa. Jemez's annual Feast Day on November 12 includes plaza dances, a trade fair, and carnival. This event is open to visitors and will be enjoyed by people interested in the contemporary life of Pueblo Indians.

Suggested reading: *The Missions of New Mexico, 1776,* by Eleanor B. Adams and Angélico Chávez. University of New Mexico Press, 1956.

Salinas National Monument

Abó

Abó, a component of Salinas National Monument, is located about 1 mile north of U.S. 60, 9 miles west of Mountainair, New Mexico.

Until recently, surface water has been the lifeblood of the arid and semiarid Southwest. The flowing spring at Abó is a reminder of why this unpretentious canyon has been the dwelling place of human beings for six centuries or more. The spring served the prehistoric Indian, nourished the conquistador, quenched the thirst of early railroad steam engines, and today supports a small Spanish-American community.

Not many yards north of Abó Spring lie the unexcavated mounds of a large Tompiro pueblo, and adjacent to it the ruins of San Gregório de Abó Mission. Abó, like Quarai and Gran Quivira, was the product of the extraordinary Franciscan missionary enterprise of the sixteenth and seventeenth centuries in New Mexico. Strategically situated between the salt lagoons east of present-day Willard and the Rio Grande pueblos, and located in an area of good piñon nut harvests, Abó was a reasonably prosperous community. It was from the sale of piñon nuts, in fact, that the mission was able to afford the purchase of a church organ in 1661.

The Abó Mission, one of seven established by the Franciscans in Las Salinas Province, dates to the 1620s. Considering the tremendous effort involved in building Abó, with its high vaults, massive sandstone walls, and heavy hand-carved timbers that were dragged down from the Manzano Mountains, it is sad to realize that its active life barely exceeded half a century. Three hundred of its three hundred and fifty-year existence has been as a ruin.

As at all the Spanish missions in the region, the relationship between the Indians of Abó and the influx of Spanish priests, soldiers, and settlers was an uncertain one. The ingredients of this relationship are so complex that they require a much longer study than the present one; however, a glimpse into the situation can be had by considering several historical facts. In 1601, the Indians from Abó, very likely in company with warriors from other pueblos in the area, fought and lost a six-day battle with a Spanish military

Abó mission complex, Salinas National Monument

force under the command of Vincente de Zaldívar. But within scarcely more than a generation, these Indians were participating in the building of the mission. And two generations later, when Abó and the rest of the Saline settlements were collapsing, many Tompiros accompanied retreating Spaniards to settlements near El Paso.

In addition to the main pueblo of Abó, situated next to the mission, a second smaller and perhaps older ruin lies further off across the arroyo that runs along the western edge of the pueblo mounds. This pueblo also is unexcavated. A rough idea of the extent of the main pueblo can be had by walking among the contours of its roomblocks and plazas. Potsherds and lithic flakes are scattered on the ground throughout a forest of cholla cacti. When Adolph Bandelier visited Abó in the late nineteenth century, he interviewed local residents who remembered seeing three standing stories in the pueblo forty years earlier.

The mission ruins were excavated and restored in the 1930s under the direction of Joseph H. Toulouse, Jr. Toulouse did not find the organ purchased through the sale of piñon nuts gathered by the Indians but did locate a kiva in the west court patio built at the same time as the church. His report also mentions the excavation of turkey pens within the mission walls and the recovery of watermelon seeds and mission grape seeds, both from the Old World. Mission grapes are associated with the vineyards of southern California, but their appearance at Abó predates their introduction to that region by over a hundred years. Domestic turkeys, of course, were an important food source of the Rio Grande pueblos prior to the arrival of the Spanish and, except for dogs, represent the only form of animal domestication in aboriginal North America. Their appearance within the Abó Mission buildings are an indication of some of the cultural benefits gained by the Spaniards in the Americas. They lost no time in introducing this important fowl to Spain, and from there it spread rapidly throughout Europe.

Presently, entrance into the Abó Mission ruin is prohibited because of the extreme instability of some of the high sandstone walls. A good view, however, can be obtained from the fence line. Abó has neither picnicking nor camping facilities. Camping is available at Manzano State Park and U.S. Forest Service areas about twenty-five miles away. Restaurants, gas stations, and stores can be found in Mountainair. The ruins of Quarai (see below) and Gran Quivira (p. 146) are within easy reach and will round out an interesting day's tour of the early Spanish missions of Las Salinas Province.

Suggested reading: *The Missions of San Gregorio de Abó,* by Joseph H. Toulouse. School of American Research, Monograph No. 13, 1949.

Quarai

Quarai is located 8 miles north of Mountainair, New Mexico, off State Highway 14. The ruins of this mission complex are part of Salinas National Monument.

An edifice in ruins, it is true, but so tall, so solemn, so dominant of that strange, lonely landscape, so out of place in that land of adobe box huts, as to be simply overpowering. On the Rhine, it would be a superlative, in the wilderness of the Manzano it is a miracle.

Charles F. Lummis,
Land of Poco Tiempo

Quarai, nestled by a cottonwood grove in a small valley near Punta de Agua, New Mexico, has survived the erosions of time and the looting of generations with strength and dignity. Its tall, massive masonry walls are still a surprise and continue to dominate the pastoral environment where they stand. The unexcavated remains of an Indian pueblo are adjacent to the mission. The pueblo, believed to have stood two or three stories high, was inhabited by Tiwa-speaking Pueblo Indians and predates the mission by several centuries. Today, Piro is the native language at Isleta and Sandia pueblos near Albuquerque.

Quarai's existence, like that of the other Saline missions, stemmed from a 1609 order from the Viceroy of New Spain to concentrate the Indian populations into fewer settlements to facilitate their administration. Construction of the Church of the Immaculate Conception and adjoining *convento* by local Indian workers under the supervision of Fray Estebán de Perea began about 1628. A much smaller church, 150 feet southwest of the ruins, predated it by about a decade. A report from about 1641 states that Quarai had a "very good church, organ and choir, very good provisions for public worship, 658 souls under its administration." It is only from such incidental comments surviving over three centuries that we can manage a glimpse of life here during the missionary period in Las Salinas.

Archaeological research carried out at this site in 1913 and 1920 focused primarily on the two churches. Findings were never formally published, and over the years most of the written records of those directing the excavations have disappeared. Archaeological material, whether in the form of recovered artifacts or written records, is subject to the same vicissitudes as the very sites from which they derive.

Geronimo de la Llana, a native of Mexico City born of Spanish and Creole parents, was Quarai's best-known priest. A reputedly virtuous man and serious educator, he developed a devoted following during the decade he ran the mission. Fray

Church of the Immaculate Conception, Salinas National Monument

Geronimo died in 1659, shortly before the quality of life at Quarai went into decline. During the subsequent century, the padre's remains were disinterred and moved three times before finding a final resting place in the crypt of St. Francis Cathedral in Santa Fe. This continual upheaval reflected the times following his death, for the next dozen years witnessed the collapse of his missionary enterprise and the disappearance of Spanish influence in the region.

Quarai's history was indeed marked by stress and conflict. Built-in tensions were exacerbated by the demands of the community's *encomendero* on the one hand and the priests on the other. Soldier-settlers felt free to establish themselves in areas under cultivation by Indians, and so great was their power that no effective complaint could be registered. Additionally, Quarai was named the regional seat of the dreaded Spanish Inquisition and became the focus of internal strife between civil, ecclesiastical, and military factions within the New Mexico colony. From a distance of more than three centuries, one can only imagine the cumulative effect all these factors must have had upon the morale and harmony of life at the mission and adjoining pueblo. It was not a situation that would generate communal strength in confronting the problems to come.

In the late 1660s, Las Salinas Province was struck by drought, crop failure, famine, and disease. If this was not sufficient, Quarai, along with Tajique, Chililí, Abó, Gran Quivira, and other outposts, was subjected to heavy attacks by Apaches and Comanches from the eastern plains. The weakened settlements soon fell. The Spanish withdrew to strongholds along the northern Rio Grande, and the Indians found refuge with related native villages also along the Rio Grande. By 1678, two years prior to the Pueblo Revolt, Quarai was a memory.

Quarai is part of Salinas National Monument and is open daily. A visitor's center, built in 1970, includes several small exhibits of historic and prehistoric artifacts and a reconstructed model of the site. An interpretive trail explains the various historic features. Visitors can picnic at tables in the shade of cottonwood trees next to the mission ruins.

Mountainair offers overnight accommodations, stores, gas stations, and restaurants. Camping areas can be found at nearby Manzano State Park and at U.S. Forest Service areas in the region. Gran Quivira (see below) and Abó (p. 142) are two nearby archaeological sites composing Salinas National Monument.

Suggested reading: *Quarai State Monument,* by John P. Wilson. Museum of New Mexico Press, 1977.

Gran Quivira

Gran Quivira is located 26 miles south of Mountainair, New Mexico, on State Highway 14.

It has never been possible to keep livestock in the said Pueblo because there is not (sufficient) water, for what there is comes only from some wells (posos) which are a quarter of a league from the place, forty or fifty estados in depth. And therefore it costs a great deal to get the water and it makes a lot of work for the Indians in obtaining it, and the wells are exhausted and there is an insufficient water supply for the people....

Nicolas de Aguilar, 1663

Water, bubbling from the ground at Abó, was so scarce at the pueblo of Gran Quivira that one wonders why anyone would have chosen such a site for their home. Located on a windy limestone bluff, Gran Quivira was inhabited by Tiwa-speaking Jumano Indians for whom life at best must have been a constant challenge.

The name Gran Quivira appears to have derived from a confusion with the destination (in present-day Kansas) of Coronado's legendary gold quest of the mid-sixteenth century. But neither the Quivira of Coronado nor that of southern Las Salinas Province produced fortune of any kind. The name Las Humanas, which appears in numerous writings, also refers to this pueblo.

Gran Quivira, a site containing seventeen multiroom house mounds, numerous kivas, a small Spanish church, and a large mission complex, was the largest of three Jumano Indian communities in the vicinity. The Jumanos no longer exist as a people, and whatever remains of their culture and history must be reconstructed from archaeological evidence and scarce historical records surviving from the seventeenth century. They were the easternmost fringe of the Pueblo Indians of Rio Grande Anasazi

Right: San Buenaventura mission, Salinas National Monument

stock, but their forebears had lived on the shifting frontier of the Mogollon to the south, and their culture reflects this influence as well.

Archaeologists have identified pithouse remains dating back to A.D. 600 to 900 in the vicinity of Gran Quivira. By A.D. 1300, Gran Quivira was a pueblo similar to those along the Rio Grande with which it had active trade relations. By the first European contact in the seventeenth century, the pueblo had become the largest in the region.

Coronado, in 1541, missed Las Salinas Province, and the Jumanos of Gran Quivira were spared Spanish contact for another fifty-seven years. In 1598, Oñate led four hundred Spaniards up the Rio Grande to a settlement near present-day San Juan and wasted no time in organizing explorations through his new-found territories. Las Humanas was discovered. One can only imagine the impression this troop of a hundred mounted men must have made upon the Jumanos, whose population was then estimated at three thousand.

The course of events at Gran Quivira paralleled in large measure that of Abó and Quarai. Gran Quivira's greater distance from Santa Fe was perhaps to its advantage, but with a more fragile economy and less hospitable environment, the Jumanos were less well-off than their neighbors, and their situation deteriorated steadily. In 1668, 450 died of starvation and were buried in shallow graves, if at all. Health and sanitary conditions were believed to have been abominable. Others were killed or enslaved by Apaches who, also under severe pressure, increased their attacks. Between 1672 and 1675, a last remnant of the original population abandoned the pueblo. Some joined more stable pueblos along the Rio Grande; others migrated south of the El Paso area. Their cultural identity was absorbed by the peoples who gave them haven.

The ruins of Gran Quivira are very impressive and well worth whatever side trip may be necessary for a visit. One will see the extensive masonry remains of the pueblo with its plazas, kivas, and roomblocks. But most striking, from an architectural standpoint, are the ruins of San Buenaventura Mission with its massive stone walls. The church itself was 128 feet long inside, which gives some idea of the size of its congregation.

The San Buenaventura excavations and repairs were begun in 1923 under the direction of Edgar Lee Hewett of Santa Fe's School of American Research, and they continued over a period of two years. In 1951, Gordon Vivian directed excavations of one kiva, the small Spanish church, and thirty-seven pueblo rooms. Later excavations were conducted by Alden Hayes.

The buried treasure legend associated with Gran Quivira was born at some point during the century following abandonment. It is a jest of history that a place so poor should be thought to contain riches. Indeed, historians have conjectured that the tales of treasure at Gran Quivira were invented by none other than the pueblo's dislocated inhabitants as a ploy for the sale of treasure maps to gullible Spaniards returning to New Mexico after reconquest. But treasure seekers over the centuries have worn themselves out in their efforts and in every case have come up empty-handed. Their enterprises, in retrospect, amounted to little more than vandalism.

Today, Gran Quivira, a national monument with a resident staff of rangers, is well protected. The National Park Service has developed a self-guiding walking tour through the ruins, and monument rangers are most helpful in supplementing the written guide with their own knowledge. The visitor center, which contains archaeological and historical exhibits, is open daily from 8:00 A. M. to 5:00 P.M., although it is not always manned in the winter. There is a picnic area and drinking water but no campground. Meals, lodging, and other services are available in Mountainair and Carrizozo.

Suggested reading: *Salinas*, School of American Research, Santa Fe, 1982.

The Cerrito Site

The Cerrito Site, 30 miles north of Espanola, New Mexico, lies just off State Highway 96 between Abiquiu Dam and Route 84.

The Chama, a tributary of the Rio Grande, flows through the wide Piedra Lumbre Valley in north-central New Mexico some sixty miles northwest of Santa Fe. Bordered by ancient river terraces and open grasslands with a backdrop of mountains, high mesas, and sandstone bluffs, the valley offers an impressive vista to travelers on New Mexico 96 and 84. This is a view that has changed little over the roughly five thousand years that human beings have been in the valley.

Perhaps the only significant geographical change to have occurred here over this long span of time is the conversion of the Rio Chama from a river to a long, sinuous lake that rises dramatically under spring run-offs. It was the construction of Abiquiu Dam at the south end of the valley and the threatened inundation of ancient sites that prompted intensive archaeological investigations in the area by the School of American Research in the late 1970s. The Cerrito Site, lying along

the reservoir shore just below the level of maximum pool, represents what is believed to be the earliest known presence of Navajo Indians in the Southwest. The site consists of the remains of a series of seventeenth-century hogans and sheep pens strung along about one hundred and fifty yards of shoreline. Although visually unimposing, this site and others in the vicinity tell a story of the valley's use by nomadic hunters and gatherers as early as 3000 B.C., of later incursions and occupations by Pueblo groups, Navajos, Utes, Comanches, Apaches, and of more recent settlement by Spanish-Americans and Anglos.

HUMAN CHRONOLOGY IN
PIEDRA LUMBRE VALLEY

3000 B.C. – A.D. 400	Archaic hunters and gatherers
400 – 1300	Use by Pueblo Indians from communities to northwest or south in Rio Grande Valley
1300 – 1350	Two Pueblo villages near present dam
1350 – 1600	Valley unoccupied
1600 – 1710	Inhabited by Navajos
1700s	Occasional presence of Utes and Comanches
Early 1800s	Settlement by Utes and Spanish-Americans
1853 – 1881	Band of Jicarilla Apaches present prior to settlement on reservations
1881 – present	Spanish-American communities and a few Anglos

The Cerrito is one of thirty-eight Navajo sites identified in the area including several villages of up to twenty-eight structures. These Navajo practiced animal husbandry (learned from the Rio Grande pueblos) and hunting and gathering. Where did they come from? As best can be reconstructed through archaeology, they were a band or clan of Apachean nomads who migrated here off the Great Plains and stayed for about a century before moving on west. Called *Apaches de Navaju* by Spanish colonists, they were first reported in the Chama Valley in 1626. They apparently lived in harmony with the Rio Grande pueblos, trading with them, adopting some of their customs, and fleeing with them after the abortive Pueblo Revolt of 1696 and ensuing Spanish military campaigns.

The U.S. Army Corps of Engineers administers the Cerrito site and maintains a campground, picnic area, and boat launching ramp near the site. Gas and groceries are available at the village of Abiquiu, and restaurants and overnight accommodations can be found in Espanola.

At the time of this writing, the Corps of Engineers is developing an interpretive trail near several stabilized hogans and animal pens at the site. In addition, artifacts, photographs, and a diorama will be exhibited at the Corps's Abiquiu Dam offices. As a ruin, Cerrito rates low on the romantic scale, but it represents a link with a most interesting period in New Mexico history. It is also the only Navajo archaeological site in the Southwest that has been set aside as a public monument.

Suggested reading: *Archaeological Studies in the Abiquiu Reservoir District,* by Curtis F. Schaafsma. In *Discovery,* School of American Research, Santa Fe, 1978.

Sandia Cave

Sandia Cave is located in a cliff in the foothills of the Sandia Mountains north of Albuquerque, New Mexico. To reach the cave from Interstate 25, take New Mexico 44 east 6 miles to Placitas and continue another 3.5 miles to a parking area and sign. From here, a well-maintained, 0.5-mile path leads to the cave.

Eighty feet up the steep eastern wall of Las Huertas Canyon in the Sandia Mountains of central New Mexico, a cave, scarcely ten feet in width, penetrates 450 feet into the limestone formation. A curiosity to hikers and picnickers, it is a place where late twentieth-century artifacts are much more in evidence than any remnant from antiquity. But in an earlier age, this long dusty tunnel into the mountain gave shelter to the oldest known race of people on the North American continent.

Sandia Cave was excavated in the late 1930s by Frank C. Hibben and a University of New Mexico archaeological crew with results that appeared to plunge the existence of man in the Southwest back twenty-five thousand years. The cave's undisturbed floor deposits contained three distinct layers of cultural material and animal bones. On the surface near the entrance were potsherds from nearby Rio Grande pueblos dating from about the twelfth century A.D. to recent times. Pueblo Indians apparently used the cave for temporary shelter while on forays into the mountains but never built any permanent dwelling under its roof.

Beneath the surface material of the cave, Hibben found a second layer containing stone tools and implements bearing a close resemblance to artifacts found at the Folsom and Clovis sites in eastern New Mexico and dating to around twelve thousand

Sandia Cave

years ago. These scrapers and spear points had been manufactured and deposited by early hunters who roamed the Great Plains and Southwest in search of big game. Lying around these Folsom points were the bone and tooth remains of such extinct North American mammals as the mammoth, ground sloth, camel, and horse. The latter two species were only reintroduced to this continent from Europe and Africa in recent history.

The Sandia Cave excavations stimulated much excitement and controversy, however, when a third and older level of cultural material underlying the Folsom layer was discovered. Hibben called these artifacts Sandia points, and their makers, Sandia man. The Sandia and Folsom layers were clearly separated by a stratum of yellow ocher deposited by water during a span of time when the cave was too wet for human use. Hibben and others dated the Sandia material to pre-twenty-five thousand years ago; more recent scientific judgment, however, has generally found this dating to be incorrect. According to present interpretations, the Folsom period of about 10,000 B.C. is more acceptable as a date for the oldest deposits of Sandia Cave. Dating methods are constantly being refined through technological advances, and it is unlikely that the Sandia controversy will soon be resolved.

Sandia Cave today offers little to see as an archaeological site and is closed to spelunkers; the Forest Service, in fact, has erected a masonry wall blocking access to the rear portion of the cave. During its long period of human use, it probably never served as a permanent dwelling nor, to the intense disappointment of archaeologists, as a burial site. But to see Sandia Cave is to fleetingly glimpse a very early chapter in the North American human story. Nomadic hunters of whom we have only the smallest knowledge knew this place well, and to enter the cave ourselves is one way of establishing contact with them.

Sandia Cave looks over a beautiful mountain canyon with a clear, fresh stream. Numerous hiking trails and picnic sites are available in the locality, and camping can be found at Coronado State Park about twelve miles west on New Mexico 44. Here also are the ruins of Kuaua (see p. 133), a large Rio Grande Pueblo site believed to have been visited by Coronado in 1540.

The Future of Antiquity in the Southwest

Village-dwelling Indians have inhabited the Southwest for at least two thousand years, leaving in their trail hundreds of thousands of archaeological sites. The sites range in type from barely noticeable scatters of stone flakes to multistoried pueblos. Whatever their individual character, many of these archaeological relics have remained undisturbed in relative obscurity and security for a long time.

As we move into the 1990s, the future of the Southwest's archaeological heritage appears increasingly uncertain. Surrounding and underlying ancient campsites, pithouses, and pueblos are vast, untapped natural resources including oil, gas, uranium, and coal. The processes involved in exploiting this mineral wealth often stand in direct opposition to efforts to preserve the region's fragile environment, including its ruins.

Running a parallel course to energy and mineral development has been population growth. Villages and cities have been expanding, roads multiplying and widening, utility lines crisscrossing long expanses, and sightseers and hikers penetrating traditionally remote areas. The result of this trend toward more people and more mobility has been, and no doubt will continue to be, increased wear and tear if not outright destruction of archaeological remains.

A third phenomenon, pothunting, has long been a major threat to archaeological preservation. With Mimbres pots currently commanding prices in excess of two thousand dollars, the temptation to pothunt on a commercial scale has become inevitable. Probe sticks and shovels have become obsolete tools in favor of bulldozers, which can churn over an entire prehistoric village site in a few hours. In recent years, unscrupulous entrepreneurs have reaped large profits at the expense of uncounted ruins. This looting of ruins, although most dramatically witnessed in southwestern New Mexico, is a serious regional and national problem.

As an issue, archaeological conservation lies in the shadow of many more publicized and pressing national problems. It has not, however, been entirely obscured. One recent significant expression of public concern was reflected in passage of the Archaeological Resources Protection Act of 1979; some excerpts from this are cited on the following pages.

It has been suggested here that growing numbers of people threaten archaeological sites; but it should be added that people can also play a key role in preservation. The new Archaeological Resources Preservation Act itself was generated by private citizens. Likewise, it was a group of concerned individuals who, in 1979, founded The Archaeological Conservancy (address: 415 Orchard Drive, Santa Fe, New Mexico 87501), a national nonprofit membership organization dedicated to preserving the best of the remaining sites of prehistoric cultures. Numerous other potentially helpful organizations — archaeological clubs, state historic preservation offices, environmental and nature groups, anthropology departments at universities, and law-enforcement agencies — can be of assistance in this area. Perhaps of greatest potential help, however, are the tens of thousands of private individuals who love the Southwest and its unique cultural heritage. These hunters, fishermen, hikers, backpackers, bird watchers, horseback riders, and others are familiar with the backcountry and can play an individually small but collectively large role as archaeological watchdogs. Working on their own initiative, but in cooperation with established organizations or agencies, they represent the potentially most effective force supporting the cause of archaeological conservation.

America's archaeological sites are a national treasure. As a collection, they are invaluable to all people, of all ethnic backgrounds, for all time. They are an inspiration to writers and artists and an irreplaceable source of knowledge to historians, social scientists, tourists, and school children. The Southwest's archaeological resources should not be carelessly destroyed for short-term gain, either by individuals or mining companies, nor should they be voraciously consumed by well-meaning archaeologists in the vanguard of energy development operations. While it would be impractical and unwise in the face of present national energy needs to assume too militant or inflexible a stance on archaeological conservation, we should nevertheless attempt to see to it that responsible compromises are made between energy requirements and cultural values. Hopefully, the present book, by generating a wider public appreciation of archaeological ruins, will have a positive influence on preserving them for the future.

Archaeological Resources Protection Act of 1979

Public Law 96-95, 96th Congress,
October 31, 1979

AN ACT

To protect archaeological resouces on
public lands and Indian lands, and for
other purposes.

*Be it enacted by the Senate and House
of Representatives of the
United States of America in Congress
assembled,*

SHORT TITLE

Section 1. This Act may be cited
as the "Archaeological Resources
Protection Act of 1979".

FINDINGS AND PURPOSE

Sec. 2 (a) The Congress finds that—
(1) archaeological resources on
public lands and Indian lands are an
accessible and irreplaceable part of
the Nation's heritage;
(2) these resources are increasingly endangered because of their
commercial attractiveness;
(3) existing Federal laws do not
provide adequate protection to pre-
vent the loss and destruction of
these archaeological resources and
sites resulting from uncontrolled
excavations and pillage; and
(4) there is a wealth of archaeological information which has been le-
gally obtained by private individuals
for noncommercial purposes and
which could voluntarily be made
available to professional archaeologists and institutions.

(b) The purpose of this Act is to
secure, for the present and future
benefit of the American people, the
protection of archaeological resources
and sites which are on public lands
and Indian lands, and to foster increased cooperation and exchange
of information between govern-
mental authorities, the professional
archaeological community, and
private individuals having collections
of archaelogical resources and data
which were obtained before the date
of the enactment of this Act.

PROHIBITED ACTS AND CRIMINAL
PENALTIES

Sec. 6 (a) No person may excavate,
remove, damage, or otherwise alter or
deface any archaeological resource located on public lands or Indian lands
unless such activity is pursuant to a
permit issued under section 4, a permit referred to in section 4(h)(2), or
the exemption contained in section
4(g)(1).
(b) No person may sell, purchase,
exchange, transport, receive, or offer
to sell, purchase, or exchange any archaeological resource if such resource
was excavated or removed from public
lands or Indian lands in violation of—
(1) the prohibition contained in
subsection (a), or
(2) any provision, rule, regulation,
ordinance, or permit in effect under
any other provision of Federal law.
(c) No person may sell, purchase,
exchange, transport, receive, or offer
to sell, purchase, or exchange, in interstate or foreign commerce, any
archaeological resource excavated,

removed, sold, purchased, exchanged, transported, or received in
violation of any provision, rule, regulation, ordinance, or permit in
effect under State or local law.

(d) Any person who knowingly
violates, or counsels, procures,
solicits, or employs any other person
to violate, any prohibition contained
in subsection (a), (b), or (c) of this
section shall, upon conviction, be
fined not more than $10,000 or
imprisoned not more than one year,
or both; *Provided, however,* that if
the commercial or archaeological
value of the archaeological resources
involved and the cost of restoration
and repair of such resources exceeds
the sum of $5,000, such person shall
be fined not more than $20,000 or
imprisioned not more than two years,
or both. In the case of a second or
subsequent such violation upon conviction such person shall be fined not
more than $100,000, or imprisoned
not more than five years, or both.

REWARDS; FORFEITURE

Sec. 8. (a) Upon the certification of
the Federal land manager concerned,
the Secretary of the Treasury is directed to pay from penalties and fines
collected under section 6 and 7 an
amount equal to one-half of such penalty or fine, but not to exceed $500,
to any person who furnishes information which leads to the finding of a civil
violation, or the conviction of criminal
violation, with respect to which such
penalty or fine was paid. If several
persons provided such information,
such amount shall be divided among
such persons. No officer or employee
of the United States or of any State
or local government who furnishes
information or renders service in
the performance of his official duties
shall be eligible for payment under this
subsection.

DESIGNED BY NANCY SOLOMON

COMPOSED IN MERGENTHALER UNIVERS

WITH YORK DISPLAY TYPE

AT THE PRESS IN THE PINES

 NORTHLAND PRESS